In Contempt
of Congress

Recent Titles in the
Praeger Series in Political Communication
Robert E. Denton, Jr., General Editor

Public Diplomacy and International Politics: The Symbolic Constructs of
Summits and International Radio News
Robert S. Fortner

The 1992 Presidential Campaign: A Communication Perspective
Edited by Robert E. Denton, Jr.

The 1992 Presidential Debates in Focus
Edited by William N. Elwood

Public Relations Inquiry as Rhetorical Criticism: Case Studies of Corporate
Discourse and Social Influence
Edited by William N. Elwood

Bits, Bytes, and Big Brother: Federal Information Control in the
Technological Age
Shannon E. Martin

Warriors' Words: A Consideration of Language and Leadership
Keith Spencer Felton

Electronic Magazines: Soft News Programs on Network Television
William C. Spragens

Political Campaign Communication: Principles and Practices, Third Edition
Judith S. Trent and Robert V. Friedenberg

Candidate Images in Presidential Elections
Edited by Kenneth L. Hacker

Earthtalk: Communication Empowerment for Environmental Action
Edited by Star A. Muir and Thomas L. Veenendall

The Clinton Presidency: Images, Issues, and Communication Strategies
Edited by Robert E. Denton, Jr. and Rachel L. Holloway

Politics, Media, and Modern Democracy: An International Study of
Innovations in Electoral Campaigning and Their Consequences
Edited by David L. Swanson and Paolo Mancini

In Contempt
of Congress

Postwar Press Coverage
on Capitol Hill

Mark J. Rozell

Praeger Series in Political Communication

Westport, Connecticut
London

Library of Congress Cataloging-in-Publication Data

Rozell, Mark J.
    In contempt of Congress : postwar press coverage on Capitol Hill /
Mark J. Rozell.
        p.   cm.—(Praeger series in political communication, ISSN
1062–5623
    Includes bibliographical references and index.
    ISBN 0–275–95690–3 (alk. paper)
    1. Press and politics—United States. 2. United States.
Congress—Reporters and reporting. 3. Journalists—Washington
(D.C.) 4. Government and the press—United States. I. Title.
II. Series.
PN4888.P6R69 1996
071′.3′09045—dc20   96–16277

British Library Cataloguing in Publication Data is available.

Library of Congress Catalog Card Number: 96–16277
ISBN: 0–275–95690–3
ISSN: 1062–5623

First published in 1996

Praeger Publishers, 88 Post Road West, Westport, CT 06881
An imprint of Greenwood Publishing Group, Inc.

Printed in the United States of America

The paper used in this book complies with the
Permanent Paper Standard issued by the National
Information Standards Organization (Z39.48–1984).

10 9 8 7 6 5 4 3 2 1

Contents

Series Foreword *by Robert E. Denton, Jr.*   vii

Acknowledgments   xi

1. Introduction   1

2. The Era of Neglect (1946–Early 1960s)   11

3. The Era of Discovery (1965–Mid-1970s)   25

4. The Era of Cynicism I (1977–Early 1990s)   53

5. The Era of Cynicism II (1990s)   91

6. Contempt of Congress: Sources and Recommendations 127

Selected Bibliography   139

Index   141

Series Foreword

Those of us from the discipline of communication studies have long believed that communication is prior to all other fields of inquiry. In several other forums I have argued that the essence of politics is "talk" or human interaction.[1] Such interaction may be formal or informal, verbal or nonverbal, public or private but it is always persuasive, forcing us consciously or subconsciously to interpret, to evaluate, and to act. Communication is the vehicle for human action.

From this perspective, it is not surprising that Aristotle recognized the natural kinship of politics and communication in his writings *Politics* and *Rhetoric*. In the former, he establishes that humans are "political beings [who] alone of the animals [are] furnished with the faculty of language."[2] And in the latter, he begins his systematic analysis of discourse by proclaiming that "rhetorical study, in its strict sense, is concerned with the modes of persuasion."[3] Thus, it was recognized over 2,300 years ago that politics and communication go hand in hand because they are essential parts of human nature.

Back in 1981, Dan Nimmo and Keith Sanders proclaimed that political communication was an emerging field.[4] Although its origin, as noted, dates back centuries, a "self-consciously cross-disciplinary" focus began in the late 1950s. thousands of books and articles later, colleges and universities offer a variety of graduate and undergraduate coursework in the area in such diverse departments as communication, mass communication, journalism, political science, and sociology.[5] In Nimmo and Sanders' early assessment, the "key areas of inquiry" included rhetorical analysis, propaganda analysis, attitude change studies, voting studies, government and the news media, functional and systems analyses, technological changes, media technologies, campaign techniques, and research techniques.[6] In a survey of the state of the field in 1983, the same authors and Lynda Kaid found additional, more specific areas of concerns such as the presidency, political polls, public opinion, debates, and advertising to name a few.[7] Since the first study, they also noted a shift away from the rather strict behavioral approach.

A decade later, Dan Nimmo and David Swanson argued that "political communication has developed some identity as a more or less distinct domain of scholarly work."[8] The scope and concerns of the area have further expanded to include critical theories and cultural studies. While there is no precise definition, method, or disciplinary home of the area of inquiry, its primary domain is the role, processes, and effects of communication within the context of politics broadly defined.

In 1985, the editors of *Political Communication Yearbook: 1984* noted that "more things are happening in the study, teaching, and practice of political communication than can be captured within the space limitations of the relatively few publications available."[9] In addition, they argued that the backgrounds of "those involved in the field [are] so varied and pluralist in outlook and approach. . . . it [is] a mistake to adhere slavishly to any set format in shaping the content."[10] And more recently, Nimmo and Swanson called for "ways of overcoming the unhappy consequences of fragmentation within a framework that respects, encourages, and benefits from diverse scholarly commitments, agendas, and approaches."[11]

In agreement with these assessments of the area and with gentle encouragement, Praeger established the Praeger Series in Political Communication. The series is open to all qualitative and quantitative methodologies as well as contemporary and historical studies. The key to characterizing the studies in the series is the focus on communication variables or activities within a political context or dimension. As of this writing, nearly forty volumes have been published and there are numerous impressive works forthcoming. Scholars from the disciplines of communication, history, journalism, political science, and sociology have participated in the series.

I am, without shame or modesty, a fan of the series. The joy of serving as its editor is in participating in the dialogue of the field of political communication and in reading the contributors' works. I invite you to join me.

Robert E. Denton, Jr.

NOTES

1. See Robert E. Denton, Jr., *The Symbolic Dimensions of the American Presidency* (Prospect Heights, Ill.: Waveland Press, 1982); Robert E. Denton, Jr., and Gary Woodward, *Political Communication in America* (New York: Praeger, 1985; 2nd ed., 1990); Robert E. Denton, Jr., and Dan Han, *Presidential Communication* (New York: Praeger, 1986); and Robert E. Denton, Jr., *The Primetime Presidency of Ronald Reagan* (New York: Praeger, 1988).

2. Aristotle, *The Politics of Aristotle*, trans. Ernest Barker (New York: Oxford University Press, 1970), p. 5.

3. Aristotle, *Rhetoric*, trans. Rhys Roberts (New York: the Modern Library, 1954), p. 22.

4. Dan Nimmo and Keith Sanders, "Introduction: The Emergence of Political Communication as a Field," in *Handbook of Political Communication*, ed. Dan Nimmo and Keith Sanders (Beverly Hills, Calif.: Sage, 1981), pp. 11–36.

5. Ibid., p. 15.

6. Ibid., pp. 17–27.

7. Keith Sanders, Lynda Kaid, and Dan Nimmo, eds., *Political Communication Yearbook: 1984* (Carbondale: Southern Illinois University, 1985), pp. 283–308.

8. Dan Nimmo and David Swanson, "The Field of Political Communication: Beyond the Voter Persuasion Paradigm," in *New Directions in Political Communication*, ed. David Swanson and Dan Nimmo (Beverly Hills, Calif.: Sage, 1990), p. 8.

9. Sanders, Kaid, and Nimmo, *Political Communication Yearbook: 1984*, p. xiv.

10. Ibid.

11. Nimmo and Swanson, "The Field of Political Communication," p. 11.

Acknowledgments

This book benefited from the efforts of a number of people and organizations. Uyen Ly and Michael Toppa (Georgetown University) and Carey Macdonald (the Brookings Institution) provided excellent research assistance. Thomas Mann, James Schneider (the Brookings Institution), Norman Ornstein (the American Enterprise Institute), and Danielle Vinson and Daniel Lipinski (formerly of Duke University Graduate School) read and commented on earlier versions of the manuscript. Grants from the Brookings Institution and the Dirksen Congressional Center funded the project.

In Contempt
of Congress

Chapter One

Introduction

In the 1994 elections, voters registered their strong discontent with representative government by choosing a new, Republican-led Congress. To many partisans, the elections results were nothing less than revolutionary—a fundamental transformation in governing philosophy. Republicans claimed that the public had repudiated decades of Democratic leadership and embraced the conservative vision of a smaller government. GOP analysts suggested that the "Contract with America"—the party's ten-point pledge for policy change—had given the public a meaningful choice in 1994 and that the voters had chosen the Republican vision.

A careful review of the polling data revealed a more complicated explanation. Voters were disgusted in general with Congress's performance. They did not believe that representative government worked for them. For example, a June 1994 *Washington Post*/ABC poll found that "the 103d Congress is seen as a do-nothing assemblage of quarrelsome partisans more attuned to the special interests than to its constituents."[1] People also perceived incumbent politicians—Democratic members of Congress and Bill Clinton—as having failed to fulfill the promise of the 1992 elections for more positive governmental action and an end to "gridlock" in Washington. The public consequently blamed the Democratic leadership and in 1994 voted once again for change.

Yet citizens reserved judgment on whether the GOP had the answers to what ailed the country. Indeed, a preelection Wirthlin Group poll found that only 4 percent of the electorate had both heard of the GOP's Contract with America—in which each candidate pledged, if elected, to vote on ten key initiatives during the first hundred days of the 104th Congress—and approved of it. Some polls showed that the more that voters became familiar with the items in the Contract, the less likely they were to vote Republican. As scholar Clyde Wilcox concluded, these results refuted the argument that voters delivered a mandate for the Contract in 1994.[2]

In 1995, the GOP leadership in the House of Representatives tried to move forward a number of the policy changes that the party had pledged to voters in the previous year. Among the pledges in the GOP Contract were votes on term limits for members of Congress, a balanced-budget amendment, and a requirement that federal employment laws imposed on private companies also be applied to Congress and its staff. Polls in early 1995 showed that much of the public was pleased that the GOP was acting to fulfill its campaign pledges.[3] Nonetheless, later polls showed once again that when people became familiar with the Contract's provisions, they expressed less support for the GOP-led Congress.

Although the House acted on nine of the ten pledges during the first hundred days of the 104th Congress, most Contract items stalled in the Senate. By the end of 1995, the GOP had accomplished little substantive legislative change, the president and Congress remained stalemated over a budget impasse that had led to the longest federal government shutdown ever, and numerous polls revealed that the public had lost patience with the new GOP leadership in Congress. The public assigned principal blame for the budget impasse to the Republican-led Congress, not President Clinton.

The public's low regard for the new congressional leadership after just one session reflected a general skepticism toward the legislative branch and impatience with the pace of change in Washington. This phenomenon was nothing new. Indeed, an ABC News poll in 1992 revealed that the public was disgusted with incumbent politicians, wanted change in Washington, and by about a 2–1 margin blamed the Republican Party for what was wrong in the nation. The same poll in 1994 found that the public was still disgusted with incumbents, demanded change, and by about a 2–1 margin largely blamed the Democratic party for the nation's ills.

Although there is no evidence that this volatility of public opinion will end anytime soon, one constant is evident in the polling data: people loathe Congress. Regardless of partisan control or the direction of policy, the public strongly registers its disapproval of Congress and its members. A 1993 poll asked respondents to rank the honesty and ethical standards of people by their professions. U.S. Senators ranked 18 percent favorable, just 2 percentage points better than lawyers and television talk-show hosts and substantially lower than funeral directors and reporters.[4]

To be sure, members of Congress bear some responsibility for the low esteem in which the public now holds them. Recent scandals involving such major figures as former senator Bob Packwood (R–Oreg.) and conflict-of-interest charges surrounding such leaders as House Speaker Newt Gingrich (R–Ga.) have reinforced the worst impressions that people have of our elected representatives. During the 1995–1996 budget stalemate, reports that numerous members had planned expensive travels abroad while the federal government was partially closed infuriated constituents.

Members frequently bad-mouth the institution, further fueling negative public perceptions. A blue-collar worker elected to the House in 1994 struck a popular chord when he said of service in Congress, "No job is beneath me."[5] Partisans frequently use the slightest hint of unethical conduct as a weapon to discredit their opponents. Candidates for Congress use negative advertising appeals to exaggerate claims of impropriety on the part of their opponents. Imagine the esteem in which we would hold the airline industry if carriers frequently ran ads accusing each other of losing baggage, missing arrival times, and engaging in unsafe practices that endanger the public: "Unreliable. Unsafe. You just can't trust Eagle Airlines."

Nonetheless, image and reality diverge widely. Members of Congress are more scrupulously attentive to enforcing ethical standards and avoiding conflicts-of-interest than ever before. The overwhelming majority of members are both ethical and conscientious lawmakers. As congressional scholars have pointed out, the public perception is that Congress is more corrupt today than at any time in our history, whereas the reality is that the Congress is more devoid of corruption than ever before. The cases of Packwood, Gingrich, and others are the exception in Congress, not the rule.

I recall attending a speech by reporter David Broder in which he asserted the thesis that Congress is routinely judged too harshly by his colleagues and the public. To the surprise of many in the audience, Broder further stated that not only was Congress a highly competent and ethical institution, but that the top 535 people from any profession—business, academia, journalism—could not exceed the overall quality and character of the people serving in the Congress.[6]

Why does the public continue to harbor such a negative view of Congress? One explanation is that people expect conflicting things from the institution and its members. For example, citizens perceive Congress as both too beholden to interest groups and out of touch with the public it serves. People demand expensive government programs, better quality delivery of public services, and lower taxes. They want Congress to be responsive, to articulate various constituents' views, yet they implore members to put an end to partisan squabbling. Constituents demand an end to pork-barrel spending, except when it benefits them. A 1994 ABC poll found that despite widespread complaints about such congressional perks as travel budgets and franked mail, 93 percent responded that their own member should try to keep constituents informed through district visits or newsletters, and despite complaints about special interests and congressional pork, 73 percent said that their own member should try to direct more federal projects to their district.[7]

During the Vietnam era, many criticized Congress for letting the president set foreign and military policy. When Congress challenged presidential authority abroad during the Reagan-Bush era, many complained of legislators undermining the powers of the chief executive and harming U.S. stature.

Another problem is that the public does not know very much about the Congress and its activities. In mid-1995, only half of the public could identify Newt Gingrich as the Speaker of the House, even though he had received enormous coverage. Yet two-thirds of the public could identify Lance Ito, the judge presiding over the double-murder trial of former football player O. J. Simpson. Only four in ten were familiar with the Contract with America, and only one-half knew that Congress had passed the landmark North American Free Trade Agreement (NAFTA).[8] It is not surprising that people harbor inaccurate perceptions of an institution about which they know very little.

What is even more surprising is that in recent years, those segments of the public that have the most knowledge of the Congress have been most hostile to the institution. For years, pollsters had found that an educated segment of the population provided a foundation of support for Congress and representative government even when most of the public was skeptical. More recently, as a study by Herb Asher and Mike Barr showed, although the less informed remain dubious of Congress, as people learn more about the institution they like it even less.[9]

Nonetheless, it still seems unfair, if not somewhat ironic, that the most representative of our national institutions—and the one closest to the people—remains the least regarded. In the public mind today, Congress almost cannot do anything right.

As numerous studies have shown, political life for most Americans is a mediated experience. People learn about our national institutions and leaders through the news media. As a study by Maxwell McCombs and Donald Shaw stated, people "learn how much importance to attach to an issue or topic from the emphasis placed on it by the mass media."[10] If Congress is held in such low esteem, there is no doubt that much of this condition can be attributed to highly critical press coverage of the legislative branch's activities. In recent years, congressional coverage has become increasingly negative.

To be sure, Congress has always been a favorite target for critics and comedians. Stereotypes of legislators who use public office for private gain and subvert the national interest have been a press staple since the earliest Congresses. Indeed, skepticism about the motives and activities of the nation's leaders has long been considered a necessary, and even healthful, element of representative government.

But healthy skepticism has now largely been replaced with a debilitating cynicism that potentially undermines the foundation of representative government. Recent coverage of Congress, even by the most prestigious news organizations, smells of tabloid sensationalism. The emphasis on petty scandal and conflict reinforces the worst stereotypes of dishonest, lazy, and vindictive legislators and perpetuates widespread public belief that corruption and malfeasance permeate life on Capitol Hill.

METHOD

The following analysis of the coverage of Congress is based on a comprehensive review of press commentary from three news weeklies (*Newsweek, U.S. News and World Report, Time*) and three news dailies (*New York Times, Wall Street Journal, Washington Post*) during selected important events since World War II. After reading every news analysis, editorial, and opposite-editorial-page column (by regularly featured columnists) about Congress during these periods, I have summarized and analyzed the major themes in congressional coverage.[11] As George C. Edwards explained, journalists "frame the news in themes" as a way to simplify complex events and then reinforce these themes through repetition. Thus images or stereotypes are built up that people perceive as reality.[12] Content analysis of the major themes in congressional coverage helps illuminate press perceptions of Congress, the kinds of legislative activities that generate favorable and unfavorable coverage, and changes in the nature of congressional coverage.

As the following makes clear, Congress has not always been subject to media scorn and ridicule. At times, coverage seems to improve. But greater media emphasis on and familiarity with Congress have not resulted in positive or even balanced coverage. Indeed, the trend has been toward greater and more negative scrutiny of Congress and its members. The content analysis is divided into three postwar time frames that distinguish the nature of congressional coverage.

First, the Era of Neglect (1946–early 1960s) was characterized by a lack of press interest in most of the activities of the legislative branch. In part, this lack of coverage of Congress reflected the post-FDR period of infatuation with presidential government. It also reflected the personalization of the presidency, largely brought about by FDR's commanding leadership and presence.

During the Era of Neglect, there was meager coverage of institutional changes that profoundly shaped the Congress. There was greater press interest in high-profile congressional investigations surrounding organized crime and Senator Joseph McCarthy's (R–Wisc.) censorious accusations of high-level officials with Communist leanings. Yet because of a reigning journalistic ethic of "objective" reporting, press commentary and analysis of these events were relatively thin, confined to the editorial and op-ed pages. A great deal of criticism attended the press for merely reporting McCarthy's outrageous accusations and therefore giving them credibility. The end of this era saw the onset of more probing, analytic journalism. I analyze the following important events during this period: the Legislative Reorganization Act (1946); the congressional investigations of the 1950s; and the debate over civil rights for African Americans (1957).

Second, the Era of Discovery (1965–mid-1970s) was a time of greater press interest in the legislative branch. This interest was brought on by the enormous legislative output of the 89th Congress, 1st session (1965), in which the Democratic president and Congress made major breakthroughs in social and economic policy.

Coverage of Congress during much of this period was highly positive, reflecting a strong preference for activist, progressive government. In response to the positive coverage, in 1966, fully 42 percent of the public expressed a "great deal" of confidence in the Congress.[13] The Era of Discovery culminated in the Watergate investigation, in which the legislative branch took the lead in exposing executive-branch corruption. As Congress embarked on major internal reforms to democratize its own procedures and enacted limits on presidential powers, the press occasionally praised the legislature's leadership, but complained about the slow pace of change. I analyze four major events of this era: the Great Society (1965); enactment of the ethics codes (1968); enactment of the Legislative Reorganization Act (1970); and the Watergate investigation/congressional reforms (1973–1974).

Third, the Era of Cynicism (1977–present) has been a time of increasingly critical, even hypercritical, coverage of the Congress. The pervasive post-Watergate press cynicism affected national institutions in general, Congress not excepted.

Early in this period, coverage reflected a disappointment with Congress's inability in 1977 to replicate the feats of the 89th Congress, 1st session. During the 1980s, the personalization of the presidency of Ronald Reagan dwarfed congressional coverage, which tended to be generally negative. Coverage turned highly critical in the late 1980s in reaction to proposals for congressional pay raises.

A series of overly hyped miniscandals in the early 1990s led to unprecedented hostile coverage of Congress that was seriously debilitating to the institution. The angry voter climate in part led to a historic change in Congress's leadership from Democratic to Republican in the 1994 elections. By 1994, only 8 percent of the public expressed a "great deal" of confidence in Congress.[14]

Despite initially high expectations for fundamental change, coverage of the new Congress was highly critical, especially since many of the major elements of the Contract with America did not pass. Nonetheless, the quantity of congressional coverage soared as the 1994 elections ushered in a historic change and the rise of the highly controversial Newt Gingrich (R–Ga.) as the Speaker of the House. I analyze eight major events during this period: the prospects for party governance (1977); enactment of the Reagan economic program (1981); tax reform (1986); the Iran-contra investigations (1986–1987); the federal pay raise proposal (1988–1989); the Middle East crisis (1990–1991); Congress under siege I (1991–1992); and Congress under siege II (1993–1995).

MAJOR FINDINGS

The following analysis reveals that there is a consistent disjuncture between what Congress is and what the press believes that the institution ought to be. Congressional coverage is most favorable in those rare occasions of policy activism and leadership during crises. Under normal circumstances, when congressional activity conforms to its constitutionally intended attributes of debate, delay, and inaction, negative coverage follows.

Congressional coverage today focuses on personalities, serious and petty scandals, conflict, and interbranch rivalry, often to the exclusion of process and policy. Scandal coverage in particular appears to drive much of the press's attention, reinforcing the public view of members in general as corrupt.

The press generally portrays Congress as incapable of leadership. In this view, only the president can provide leadership and direction. Congress works best under the guide of an activist, strong president.

The trend in congressional coverage has been toward an increasingly negative view of the institution. Although the press has never been strongly enamored with Congress, the nature of the more recent negative coverage goes well beyond the disjuncture between what is and what ought to be. Whereas Congress used to receive press criticism for not conforming to an idealistic press view of how the legislative process should work, much of the recent coverage can be described simply as "Congress bashing." It is one thing to portray that institution as inefficient and incapable of leadership. It is something else to portray its members as venal and corrupt.

Congress does not do a good job of protecting its own image. Individual members and the institution as a whole need to respond to the evident need to better communicate with the press and the public about the nature of the legislative process. As *Congressional Quarterly*'s Ronald Elving explained, members excel at self-presentation, but they contribute little to media and public understanding of the institution more generally.[15] The concluding chapter examines in more detail some of the most important causes of negative coverage and suggests ways in which Congress can do better at presenting and explaining its activities through the media.

NOTES

1. Richard Morin and David S. Broder, "Six Out of Ten Disapprove of Way Hill Does Its Job," *Washington Post*, July 3, 1994, pp. A1, A8.

2. Clyde Wilcox, *The Latest American Revolution? The 1994 Elections and Their Implications for Governance* (New York: St. Martin's, 1995), p. 21.

3. See Richard Morin, "Poll Numbers Up for Clinton, Congress," *Washington Post*, January 31, 1995, pp. A1, A4.

4. Survey conducted by the Gallup Organization, July 19–21, 1993, cited in Karlyn Bowman and Everett Ladd, "Public Opinion toward Congress: A Historical Look," in Thomas Mann and Norman Ornstein, eds., *Congress, the Press, and the Public* (Washington, DC: Brookings/American Enterprise Institute, 1994), p. 50.

5. Representative Mark Early (R–Fla.), quoted in *Newsweek*, December 25, 1995/January 1, 1996, p. 65.

6. Broder made these comments in a 1983 speech sponsored by the White Burkett Miller Center at the University of Virginia.

7. Richard Morin, "You Think Congress Is Out of Touch?" *Washington Post*, October 16, 1994, pp. C1, C4.

8. Howard Kurtz, "Tuning Out Traditional News," *Washington Post*, May 15, 1995, pp. A1, A6.

9. Herb Asher and Mike Barr, "Popular Support for Congress and Its Members," in Mann and Ornstein, *Congress, the Press, and the Public*, p. 19.

10. Maxwell E. McCombs and Donald L. Shaw, "The Agenda-setting Function of the Press," in Doris A. Graber, ed., *Media Power in Politics* (Washington, DC: Congressional Quarterly, 1984), p. 65.

11. The selection of national print-media sources is adopted from Stephen Hess's description of the news organization hierarchy in *The Washington Reporters* (Washington, DC: Brookings, 1981). According to Hess, there is a "solar system of Washington news gathering." This system includes "the sun," or the "political government," and the various planets, the Washington news organizations. These news organizations form "an inner ring, a ring of middle distance, and an outermost ring."

The inner ring comprises the most influential news organizations. These organizations are most important to the political government because "through them it learns what the country is learning about what it is doing." The inner-ring organizations now include the Associated Press, United Press International, American Broadcasting Company, National Broadcasting Company, Columbia Broadcasting System, *Newsweek*, *U.S. News and World Report*, *Time*, *New York Times*, *Washington Post*, and the *Wall Street Journal* (p. 24). In another study, Hess showed that press officers, in recognition of the inner ring's influence, give preferential treatment to the most prominent news media (*The Government/Press Connection* [Washington, DC: Brookings, 1984], p. 100).

This study focuses on those inner-ring sources that comprise the nucleus of Washington journalism—the print media. Hess noted that Washington news has a rhythm set by the major national news dailies (*New York Times*, *Wall Street Journal*, and *Washington Post*). This news "travels a circuitous route back into the political government and out again to the rest of the country via the electronic media" (p. 96). Print journalism thus becomes the focal point of national opinion development, and journalists become the molders of public perceptions of Congress's performance. Television networks have a "secondary impact" on the political government, and the wire services do not emphasize interpretive reporting and news analysis as much as the major print-media sources.

12. George C. Edwards, *The Public Presidency: The Pursuit of Popular Support* (New York: St. Martin's, 1983), pp. 159, 166.

13. Robert J. Samuelson, "Great Expectations," *Newsweek*, January 8, 1996, p. 32.

14. Ibid.

15. Ronald D. Elving, "Brighter Lights, Wider Windows: Presenting Congress in the 1990s," in Mann and Ornstein, *Congress, the Press, and the Public*, pp. 171–206.

Chapter Two

The Era of Neglect
(1946–Early 1960s)

During the Era of Neglect, coverage of Congress was sparse, judgmental commentary even more so. Several contributing factors were at work. First, the leading press generally operated under the rules of objectivity. Many considered opinion-laden coverage unprofessional and demanded that facts merely be reported. Consequently, the extensive daily judgmental commentary about leaders and institutions so widely practiced today simply did not then exist.

Second, the preference for straightforward reporting meant a lack of the kind of cynical coverage of Congress seen today. Despite lower ethical standards for public officials and the known presence of some questionable figures in Congress, there was little scandal-driven coverage. For good or bad, practices that would make repeated front-page headlines today hardly raised eyebrows during this time.

Third, this era represented a time of infatuation with a strong, progressive-oriented presidency. Opinion leaders in the early post-FDR years were enamored of presidential power and tended to see Congress as an obstructionist institution that too often impeded progress. During the Eisenhower years, the elites expressed a preference for stronger presidential leadership in the FDR mold. They rarely looked to Congress to take on the leadership that they perceived lacking in the White House.

This chapter examines press coverage of Congress during the following important events that merited press scrutiny: the Legislative Reorganization Act of 1946, congressional investigations of the 1950s, and legislative action in civil rights during 1957.

LEGISLATIVE REORGANIZATION ACT (1946)

Because of the enormous expansion of executive-branch powers during Franklin D. Roosevelt's administration, many members of Congress recognized a need for reform of the legislative branch.[1] Scholars too urged changes to strengthen Congress. As a 1945 report by the American Political Science Association stated:

Congress must modernize its machinery and methods to fit modern conditions if it is to keep pace with a greatly enlarged and active executive branch. This is a better approach than that which seeks to meet the problem by reducing and hamstringing the executive. A strong and more representative legislature, in closer touch with and better informed about the administration, is the antidote to bureaucracy.[2]

In 1945, the House and Senate established a Joint Committee on the Organization of Congress to include six members from each chamber (divided equally by party). The Congress named Senator Robert M. La Follette, Jr., as committee chairman and Representative A. S. Mike Monroney as vice chairman. The committee considered many reform proposals. Among those left out of the final report were that seniority not be the basis for selecting committee chairmen, that some of the powers of the House Committee on Rules be curtailed, and that debate in the Senate more easily be limited. President Harry S Truman signed the Legislative Reorganization Act of 1946 on August 2, and even though it left out these proposals, it did include substantial reforms.

Among the most important reforms were (1) reducing the number of committees in each chamber by more than half; (2) directing standing committees to maintain complete records of hearings; (3) opening committee hearings to the public, except mark-up or executive sessions; (4) creating a Joint Budget Committee to prepare the legislative budget; (5) reducing the workload by limiting categories for the introduction of private bills; (6) adding staff to standing committees; (7) increasing the salary of members by 25 percent beginning in 1947; and (8) requiring lobbyists to register and report their expenditures.[3]

The act also strengthened congressional oversight and investigative authority by stating the intention to have investigations carried out primarily by standing committees rather than by specially created ones, and it called for continuous oversight of programs rather than occasional hearings.

During debate of the Legislative Reorganization Act, *Newsweek* columnist Raymond Moley offered a common postwar criticism of Congress: "Its organization and methods of operation do not correspond to the vital interests of the nation." He continued, "There are committees which are pure anachronisms," and "there are other committees whose duties are so heterogeneous that their names no longer have meaning. And the seniority system has placed utter misfits in many chairmanships. There are, in fact, too many committees in both houses." "We cannot," he concluded, "expect Congress to regain its lost influence until it modernizes itself."[4]

The rest of the press agreed on the necessity of congressional reform and the reasons for that necessity and extolled the virtues of the changes that Congress enacted. The *New York Times* praised the reform proposals of the La Follette–Monroney committee as "some helpful suggestions for bringing our stagecoach congressional procedures into closer harmony with the airplane age." The *Times* believed that "there should be little opposition to these proposals either on Capitol Hill or off of it" because of the "harassing clutter of detail" that members of Congress had to sift through to do their jobs. The *Times* agreed that the members needed staff assistance and more efficient organization to perform their duties. The editorial only criticized the committee for not changing the seniority system responsible for chairmanships of standing committees.[5]

After Congress adopted the reforms, the *Times* again praised the effort. "Although it did not achieve in a single step all the reforms needed, Congress has sent to the White House a reorganization bill that assures much self-improvement." The editorial approved of the congressional pay-raise proposal and acknowledged that the legislators had been "underpaid." Indeed, the *Times* emphasized the responsibilities of serving in Congress and the need for "the kind of men and women we want to attract to that office." Although the bill was not perfect, "it is a beginning and a good one. Congress members should now be able to do their jobs more creditably, and, having less anxiety over their personal pocketbooks, can confine their attention more fully to the essential business of making the nation's laws."[6]

The *Washington Post* reacted similarly to the committee's reform proposals:

Considering the remarkable achievements of the Committee on the Organization of Congress, we are not inclined to carp about its failure to bring in a plan to abolish the seniority rule or clip the wings of the arbitrary Rules Committee in the House. . . . In our opinion, accordingly, the public interest can best be served by concentrating full attention upon the progressive and intelligent reforms it has proposed by almost unanimous agreement, and forget for the time being about any inevitable sins of omission.[7]

The *Post* also later praised the reform bill adopted by the Congress, including the proposal to increase congressional salaries:

> The hike in the remuneration of our legislators is an integral part of the modernization of Congress. They are underpaid in terms of their responsibilities and commitments. . . . The hemorrhage of public servants out of the Government has become dangerous to good administration. . . . It is caused for no other reason than that the officials can no longer afford to work for the Government.

The *Post* noted that the streamlining of legislative procedure was most welcome given Congress's dilatory performance before and during the war in providing credit to Great Britain and enacting a new Office of Price Administration:

> Congratulations are the due of Congress for streamlining its creaking and groaning machinery. It is . . . a miracle that such a seven-league step has been taken in the reorganization of Congress. All through the war Congress refused to follow the lead of the country and undergo reconversion in the interest of efficient operation. . . . With the valiant generalship of Senator La Follette and Representative Monroney, they have helped to make the Seventy-ninth Congress memorable, and in future there should be fewer of those snarls in Congress which have recently been productive of jeremiads about the imminence of a constitutional crisis.[8]

The *Wall Street Journal* referred to the reform bill as one of Congress's positive accomplishments in 1946 and pointed out that the reform measures had "not generally received the notice that their importance deserves." The paper particularly congratulated Congress for adopting such important reform measures "without executive inspiration or executive pressure."[9]

A *U.S. News* report noted that Congress had become a burdensome place to serve, not "as glamorous as it looked to the people back home." The report added that the reforms made "the new Congress" a "pleasanter place to work."[10]

Like most of the press corps, Marquis Childs of the *Post* lauded the initial committee report as an "excellent" piece of work that addressed urgent needs. Childs criticized Congress for not addressing the seniority system, which was one of the "defects . . . of the process of democracy in this country," but applauded the recommendation to provide a pension system to its members. The reforms offered "a long step toward bringing our government up to the times."[11]

After Senate passage of the bill, Raymond Moley urged readers to pressure House members to also pass the reforms, summing up the bill as the "most constructive measure to improve the efficiency of the national legislature that has appeared in a hundred years." He argued,

> Since the basis of efficiency is the individual member, the bill not only makes congressional service more attractive to able men and women, but increases the services at the disposal of each member. . . . Members' and officers' salaries are increased, as they should be. And, to promote security and to encourage the retirement of the superannuated, a pension system is created.
>
> It is absurd to expect a Congress which spends billions and imposes regulations upon all aspects of our life to operate through antique methods and to be niggardly about providing itself with working tools. We shall have better congressmen and better legislation only when service in Congress becomes more attractive to exceptional people.[12]

Despite their groundbreaking nature, the congressional reforms of 1946 did not receive undue attention from the press, even though the leading newspapers and news magazines certainly did not ignore the effort. But as a *Wall Street Journal* editorial noted, the reform measures did not receive "the notice that their importance deserves."[13] Raymond Moley noted that "public interest goes to the sensational and bizarre in Congress. But incompetence costs more than a thousand scandals."[14] The lack of coverage and analysis lends credibility to the belief that the press does not adequately cover stories concerning process and institutional development.

What press coverage there was, however, was positive.[15] From today's vantage, it is noteworthy that the press favored such proposals as the congressional pay raise and pension plan. The press portrayed work in Congress as an honorable form of public service, often less than glamorous, and deserving of the kinds of financial rewards that would attract the best-qualified representatives. The press also strongly endorsed the modernization of the committee structure. What criticism there was focused on the failure to reform the seniority system. The more extensive reform agenda would have to wait.

CONGRESSIONAL INVESTIGATIONS OF THE 1950s

Although press attention to Congress during this period remained negligible, interest in legislative activity picked up during investigations of organized crime and alleged Communist infiltration of the federal government. To paraphrase Moley, press interest turned to the sensational and the bizarre.

In 1951, the Senate Crime Investigation Committee, chaired by Senator Estes Kefauver (D–Tenn.), held secret and open hearings throughout the country on organized crime. The purposes of the hearings were to uncover criminal activities and recommend measures to combat the problem.

Because a number of the hearings featured well-known notorious crime figures and were broadcast by radio and television, public interest in the inquiries was unusually high. News reports noted that retail outlets complained of slackened sales due to the public fixation with the hearings.

Press coverage of the inquiries was extensive and mostly descriptive. News stories detailed revelations from the hearings and covered such controversies as whether public broadcasting violated witnesses' privacy rights[16] and whether the committee's tenure should be extended to allow for additional hearings.[17] The *New York Times* ran detailed excerpts from the testimony at the hearings.[18]

Some news headlines characterized the hearings as a "circus" and a "show," suggesting some judgment of the committee's purpose.[19] Some columnists questioned whether the hearings would have any serious impact on organized crime in the long run, also suggesting that publicity rather than substantive achievement was the committee's goal.[20]

Nonetheless, most agreed that government action to combat crime was a worthy endeavor. The *Washington Post* and the *New York Times*, for example, ran a number of editorials praising the committee findings and the educative role of the hearings.[21] There was little press criticism of the committee and no controversy over the largely nonjudgmental nature of the coverage. Controversy arose instead over the factual reporting of the outlandish charges of a U.S. senator who headed another congressional investigation.

On March 9, 1950, Senator Joseph McCarthy (R–Wisc.) made a speech in Wheeling, West Virginia, during which he alleged that Communists and former Communists had infiltrated the federal government. McCarthy created a national firestorm by pressing these baseless allegations for several years.

McCarthy made his accusations during a period in which "objective" coverage remained the norm. His statements were considered newsworthy by the press because he was an official source who claimed to have knowledge of a widespread conspiracy.

The trouble was that most journalists knew early on that McCarthy was a demagogue, and yet they did not expose him as such. Edwin Bayley's authoritative study of press coverage of McCarthy showed that the press had failed to reveal to the public important information that would have exposed the senator as a fraud.[22]

In 1953, *New York Times* editorial writer John B. Oakes said that McCarthy's success at reaching public opinion ultimately had a chilling effect on editorial opinion and commentary.[23] A majority of newspaper editors took no position on McCarthy's charges at a time when the public relied on the editorial pages for some guidance to understand the news.[24] McCarthy fully exploited his ability to influence public opinion through the uncritical media.[25]

Not all of the press was so easily intimidated or neutral. Such influential columnists as Drew Pearson, Marquis Childs, and Stewart Alsop were highly critical of McCarthy's charges and tactics.[26] Murrey Marder of the *Post* carefully examined public records to expose some of the senator's falsehoods.[27] The *Washington Post* conducted a relentless editorial campaign against the senator. The paper, according to Bayley, "deserves at least as much credit for its long struggle against McCarthy as for its Watergate triumph."[28] In the first month after McCarthy's speech at Wheeling, the *Post* ran five editorials and four syndicated columns that were highly critical of the senator. By contrast, the *New York Times* and *Wall Street Journal* together ran only three critical editorials and no syndicated columns.[29]

Bayley concluded that, "McCarthy's tactics produced lasting changes in the media. Newspaper people realized that it was not enough simply to tell what had happened or what was said, but that they had to tell what it meant and whether or not it was true. By 1954, interpretive reporting and news analysis had become standard practice; these functions were no longer left to the editorial writers."[30] Bernard Roschco confirmed that McCarthyism precipitated a reexamination of reportorial techniques, leading some in the press to extol the responsibility to examine causes of events and offer interpretations. That meant extending the privilege of commentary to reporters as well as editors and columnists. News analysts became more pervasive and took on greater prominence in the press.[31] These changes in part also precipitated the rise of a more progressive and reformist press not afraid to lead the charge on issues of social and economic justice. The press ultimately played a central role in the nation's progress in civil rights.

CONGRESS AND CIVIL RIGHTS (1957)

The 85th Congress, 1st session, produced a compromise voting-rights law that won plaudits from the press. Although no one considered the measure ideal by any standard, editorial and opinion commentary lauded Congress for making an important, positive step in the right direction.

Passage of the legislation was not easy, and many initially wondered whether Congress ultimately would fail to act. Southern senators had successfully used the filibuster on a number of occasions to thwart civil rights legislation. Rule XXII, enacted by the Senate in 1949, made it almost impossible to limit debate in the chamber. It required 64 senators present to vote to end debate to break a filibuster. Although the House had passed the voting-rights measure relatively quickly in the 85th Congress, it initially appeared that southern opposition in the Senate would thwart the effort.

The measure that Congress adopted near the end of the session established a federal civil rights division in the Justice Department. It gave the attorney general the power to intervene in cases of voting-rights abuses and authorized federal judges to issue injunctions in such instances.

When the 85th Congress convened, there were few high hopes for major accomplishment. The *Washington Post* editorialized that divided government—Republican president, Democratic Congress—limited the potential for real legislative gains.[32] The *New York Times* expressed similar concern but worried even more about the potential impact of "that vicious and anti-democratic device known as the filibuster."[33]

At the four-month stage of the session (April), the *Times* blasted Congress for its "virtually negligible" record. The editorial urged quick action in such areas as civil rights, education, and immigration.[34] It also invited a strong rebuke from Senate Majority Leader Lyndon Johnson (D–Tex.), who claimed that the session had thus far produced a good record. The *Times* returned the fire, citing the allegedly weak record of "just two major pieces of legislation" in four months. It listed numerous major policy initiatives that Congress presumably should have moved forward.[35] Two months later the paper lamented that after six months of toiling on Capitol Hill, members of Congress had "very little to show for it."[36] One month later the *Times* complained of "urgent matters" not receiving serious-enough treatment in the Senate.[37] A

Times reporter later added that the House was becoming a weak rubber-stamp body that moved too slowly to reform its arcane procedures.[38]

These harsh judgments occurred during a period in which the fate of the major civil rights initiative remained in doubt. The House passed the measure favored by the Eisenhower administration 286–126. The Senate became nearly deadlocked over certain provisions of the legislation strongly opposed by southern members. The *Washington Post* urged positive Senate action because "the eyes of the world [were] upon it," and denying blacks their voting rights "would be a blow to the whole free world."[39]

To save the measure, Senate Majority Leader Johnson forged a compromise proposal that was agreeable to both southern and northern members, and consequently his effort avoided a filibuster. The compromise allowed for a jury-trial amendment to the bill that mollified southern members who expressed concern about possible federal judicial actions. To be sure, civil rights advocates and numerous editorials lamented that the amendment watered down the legislation significantly, but they maintained that some progress on civil rights was better than no action at all. The *Post* said better to take "three fourths of a loaf" rather than no bread at all.[40] The *Times* editorialized "half a loaf, or a thin slice of a loaf is probably better than no bread."[41]

Walter Lippmann considered the jury-trial amendment a "mistake," but he too urged adoption of the legislation. "For the bill is not only a great advance in the civil rights of the Southern Negroes. It is a very great advance in the concurrence on a dangerous issue of the Nation as a whole."[42]

The *Post* described the eventual decision by congressional leaders to accept compromise as "an act of genuine statesmanship" and "a masterful achievement."[43] The *Times* agreed and added that the agreement to compromise may have "proved that the Senatorial roadblock to remedial legislation is not completely impassable."[44]

At the end of the legislative session, after passage of the voting-rights law, the *Post* again lauded Congress's "remarkable achievement" and "the essence of constructive leadership."[45] Furthermore, "If the act is wisely administered, it alone will give the Eighty-fifth Congress a niche in our national history."[46] The *Times* called the law "incomparably the most significant domestic action of any Congress in this century."[47]

Many credited the achievement to Johnson's astute leadership. The *Times* praised his efforts to get southern members to "break with the past and to bring this bill through—half-loaf or not—to a bipartisan victory for the sense of justice that moving history demands."[48] The *Post* called the achievement "a personal triumph for Sen. Lyndon Johnson" and "leadership of a high order."[49] Arthur Krock praised Johnson's "extraordinary success," and William S. White wrote that "the story of the first session of the Eighty-fifth Congress to an uncommon degree has been the story of Senator Lyndon B. Johnson of Texas."[50] White maintained that Congress had reestablished itself as the nation's leading lawmaking branch after having earlier ceded many of its powers to the president. He lauded the passage of such Democratic initiatives as the voting-rights law during a period of Republican control of the executive.[51]

Passage of the first major civil rights initiative since Reconstruction resulted in highly favorable coverage of the Congress and its leadership. The press commentary evidenced a strong preference for an activist Congress that enacted progressive reforms. Not only was progressive action in civil rights good for the country, many suggested that institutional reforms designed to make Congress more efficient were desirable.

NOTES

1. The background section is summarized from various news reports; Congressional Quarterly, *Origins and Development of Congress* (Washington, DC: Congressional Quarterly, 1976); and Walter J. Oleszek, *Congressional Procedures and the Policy Process* (Washington, DC: Congressional Quarterly, 1978).

2. *The Reorganization of Congress.* A Report of the Committee on Congress of the American Political Science Association (Washington, DC: Public Affairs Press, 1945), pp. 80–81.

3. Congressional Quarterly, *Origins and Development of Congress*, pp. 136–138.

4. Raymond Moley, "What Does Congress Represent?" *Newsweek*, May 27, 1946, p. 100.

5. "Rip Van Winkle Wakes Up," *New York Times*, March 10, 1946, sec. 4, p. 8.

6. "For a Stronger Congress," *New York Times*, July 28, 1946, sec. 4, p. 8.

7. "Make It One Package," *Washington Post*, March 12, 1946, p. 6. See also "Fiscal Controls," *Washington Post*, March 14, 1946, p. 8; "Undermining Reform," *Washington Post*, September 30, 1946, p. 6.

8. "Unsnarling Congress," *Washington Post*, July 30, 1946, p. 10. The *Post* featured an opposite-editorial column by George B. Galloway, chairman of the Committee on Congress of the American Political Science Association, extolling the reform bill as "an epochal forward step toward congressional self-improvement. . . . Congress has accomplished a miracle. In one courageous leap our national legislature has jumped the hurdles of timidity, inertia, and vested interests and approved modernization of much of its antiquated machinery and methods."

George B. Galloway, "Reorganization Achievement," *Washington Post*, July 30, 1946, p. 4.

9. "Congress's Achievement," *Wall Street Journal*, July 30, 1946, p. 4. See also "A Promise to Be Kept," *Wall Street Journal*, October 29, 1946, p. 6.

10. "Congressmen's Streamlined Job: Pensions, Pay Raise, More Help," *U.S. News and World Report*, August 9, 1946, pp. 14–15.

11. Marquis Childs, "Revamping Congress," *Washington Post*, March 16, 1946, p. 6.

12. Raymond Moley, "How You Can Get a Better Congress," *Newsweek*, July 8, 1946, p. 92.

13. "Congress's Achievement," p. 4.

14. Moley, "How You Can Get a Better Congress," p. 92.

15. One news story surveyed press reactions to the reforms from around the country. It found overwhelming endorsement of the reform proposals passed by Congress and some criticism for not reforming the seniority system and for not abolishing the Senate filibuster as well as for increasing congressional pay (some thought the pay increase not substantial enough to attract top-quality people to government, and some extolled the ideal of public service as a reward in itself that does not offer financial gain too). See "Changes in the Organization of Congress: Press Reactions," *U.S. News and World Report*, August 9, 1946, p. 21. Of the press surveyed here, one news article did not express enthusiasm for the reform proposals. That article referred to the proposals as "a series of mild recommendations aimed at clearing away some of the congressional deadwood, modernizing operations and giving Congress better equipment to do its job." The article noted the lack of reform proposals of the seniority system and the House Committee on Rules. See "Plan for Remaking Congress: Coming Fight against Change," *U.S. News and World Report*, March 15, 1946, p. 20.

16. Jay Walz, "Court Ruling Seen on TV in Hearings," *New York Times*, February 26, 1951, p. 15; William M. Blair, " 'Outraged' over Video at Hearing, Carroll, Bet Expert, Defies Senators," *New York Times*, February 25, 1951, pp. 1, 62; "Bar Group Cautions Kefauver on TV Use," *New York Times*, February 27, 1951, p. 21; James A. Hagerty, "Costello Defies Senators, Walks out of Hearing Here," *New York Times*, March 16, 1951, pp. 1, 25.

17. "New Crime Studies by Senate Opposed," *New York Times*, April 17, 1951, p. 15; "Bill Asks New Life for Crime Inquiry," *New York Times*, April 18, 1951, p. 37; C. P. Trussell, "Senate Continues Inquiry on Crime," *New York Times*, April 25, 1951, p. 24.

18. See, for example, "Excerpts from Third Day's Proceedings," *New York Times*, March 15, 1951, pp. 24–25; "Excerpts from Testimony Here on Fourth Day of Senate Committee's Inquiry into Crime," *New York Times*, March 16, 1951, p. 24.

19. "Exposure by TV," *Washington Post*, March 22, 1951, p. A10; "Televised Testimony," *Washington Post*, March 2, 1951, p. A20; "Kefauver Circus," *Newsweek*, March 12, 1951, pp. 22–23; Emanuel Perlmutter, "Slain 'Bugsy'

Siegel's Girl Friend Steals Senate Crime Inquiry Show," *New York Times*, March 16, 1951, p. 24.

20. See, for example, Raymond Moley's columns: "After Kefauver—What?" *Newsweek*, April 9, 1951, p. 92; "After Kefauver—What? (2)," *Newsweek*, April 16, 1951, p. 112; "After Kefauver—What? (3)," *Newsweek*, April 30, 1951, p. 88.

21. "The Big Show," *Washington Post*, March 21, 1951, p. A10; "The Big Show," *New York Times*, March 14, 1951, p. 32; "Climax on Foley Square," *New York Times*, March 19, 1951, p. 26; "The Captive Audience," *New York Times*, March 21, 1951, p. 32; "Court Adjourned," *New York Times*, March 22, 1951, p. 30; "The Enemy Within," *New York Times*, September 1, 1951, p. 10.

22. Edwin Bayley, *Joe McCarthy and the Press* (Madison: University of Wisconsin Press, 1981), p. 219.

23. Ibid., pp. 216–217.

24. Ibid., p. 219.

25. Ibid., p. 8.

26. Ibid., pp. 57–58.

27. Ibid., p. 215.

28. Ibid., p. 216.

29. Ibid., pp. 223–228.

30. Ibid., p. 219.

31. Bernard Roschco, "The Evolution of News Content in the American Press," in Doris A. Graber, ed., *Media Power in Politics* (Washington, DC: Congressional Quarterly, 1984), pp. 18–19.

32. "Eighty-Fifth Congress," *Washington Post*, January 3, 1957, p. A14.

33. "The Eighty-Fifth," *New York Times*, January 3, 1957, p. 32.

34. "Fourth Month," *New York Times*, April 11, 1957, p. 30.

35. "Congressional Record," *New York Times*, April 23, 1957, p. 30.

36. "Two Months to Go," *New York Times*, June 2, 1957, sec. 4, p. 10.

37. "Niagara Power Waits Again," *New York Times*, July 10, 1957, p. 26.

38. Allen Drury, "Is the House a Rubber Stamp?" *New York Times Magazine*, August 11, 1957, pp. 13, 32, 35.

39. "Big Debate Begins," *Washington Post*, July 9, 1957, p. A10. See also "Senate in a Knot," *Washington Post*, August 1, 1957, p. A18.

40. "Three Fourths of a Loaf," *Washington Post*, August 3, 1957, p. A10. See also "All or Nothing?" *Washington Post*, August 6, 1957, p. A14; "Give It a Try," *Washington Post*, August 8, 1957, p. A14; "The Stake in Civil Rights," *Washington Post*, August 2, 1957, p. A12.

41. "A Fraction of a Loaf," *New York Times*, August 7, 1957, p. 26. See also "Civil Rights: What Next?" *New York Times*, August 9, 1957, p. 18; "Half a Loaf," *New York Times*, August 17, 1957, p. 14; Marquis Childs, "Politics Spicing Civil Rights Stew," *Washington Post*, August 16, 1957, p. A14; James Reston, "Even a Slice of Bread Is Something," *New York Times*, August 4, 1957, sec. 4, p. 8.

42. Walter Lippmann, "A Strong Bill," *Washington Post*, August 8, 1957, p. A15.

43. "Victory for Everyone," *Washington Post*, August 26, 1957, p. A10.

44. "A Civil Rights Bill," *New York Times*, August 25, 1957, sec. 4, p. 8.

45. "The Country's Gain," *Washington Post*, August 31, 1957, p. A6.

46. "Eighty-fifth's First Round," *Washington Post*, September 2, 1957, p. A14.

47. "The Eighty-fifth to Date," *New York Times*, September 1, 1957, sec. 4, p. 8.

48. Ibid.

49. "Mr. Johnson's Triumph," *Washington Post*, August 10, 1957, p. A6.

50. Arthur Krock, "Senator Johnson and Some Others," *New York Times*, September 3, 1957, p. 26; William S. White, "Emergence of Johnson," *New York Times*, September 2, 1957, p. 8.

51. William S. White, "Congress Record Shows Revival of Policy Powers," *New York Times*, September 1, 1957, pp. 1, 8. Not every report was so favorable. See "The Do-Little 85th Congress," *Time*, September 9, 1957, pp. 24–25.

Chapter Three

The Era of Discovery
(1965–Mid-1970s)

During the Era of Discovery, press coverage of Congress was less negative than usual. Indeed, during the 89th Congress, 1st session (1965), the coverage was largely congratulatory. Journalists applauded the high level of legislative activism under the guiding hand of strong presidential leadership. Congress embarked on historic reforms during this era focusing on ethics (1968 and the mid-1970s) and legislative organization (1970–mid-1970s).

At certain stages, the Congress appeared capable of breaking the stalemate usually engendered by the system of separated powers. Although during the earlier postwar period, the press had shown stronger sympathy for presidential activism, journalists discovered that Congress was capable of national leadership. The Watergate period in particular showed that Congress could seize the initiative when needed. Nonetheless, despite significant legislation, reforms, and investigations, a good deal of the Congress's coverage emphasized what the institution and its members had failed to achieve.

THE GREAT SOCIETY (1965)

The first session of the 89th Congress is widely regarded as one of the most remarkable legislative periods in congressional history. Massive legislative output gave substance to President Lyndon B. Johnson's Great Society. A civil rights bill was enacted, as was a general education bill, Medicare, rent subsidies, and a constitutional amendment on presidential succession, all unsuccessfully proposed in previous administrations.

The policy activism of the session was encouraged by Johnson's landslide victory, his renowned legislative leadership, and large Democratic majorities in both chambers (295–140 in the House, 62–37 and 1 independent in the Senate). In addition, large numbers of freshman Democratic legislators (72 in the House) had been elected, many of whom owed their victories to Johnson's strength at the polls and were committed to liberal reforms and quick action on problems. Also helpful were the earlier reforms of the Rules Committee that, until reconfigured and enlarged from 12 to 15 members, had blocked many progressive proposals.

The press covered this extraordinary legislative session extensively. President Johnson's role in engineering the Great Society programs received most of the attention and credit, but considerable coverage also focused on Congress.

If any Congress since World War II could be presented as a reporter's model of the ideal, the 1965 legislative session has to be it. The *New York Times* referred to the 89th Congress as "the best Congress since World War II";[1] the *Washington Post* pointed to "a great record of achievement";[2] and others grasped at laudatory observations: "miracle," "revolution," "worldwide significance," "outstanding record," "massive," "distinguished," "extraordinary," "remarkable," "remarkably productive," "remarkable achievements," "historic significance," and "matchless in our time."

Some criticized Congress for not going further, for not enacting home rule for the District of Columbia or repealing the federal code that permits states to enact right-to-work laws. A few also complained that it had not aggressively pursued legislative reform—particularly of the seniority system. The *Wall Street Journal* expressed reservations about the Great Society programs being enacted at such a frenetic pace. But the *Journal* was one of only a few voices raised against the fast pace. Other press criticisms emphasized the need for Congress to do more than it had—hardly criticisms at all.

At the opening of the 89th Congress, the *New York Times* speculated that the first legislative session would be very productive. Because of the resounding vote of confidence that the public had given to the Democrats in 1964, the president and Congress had a rare opportunity to work together. The *Times* revealed a preference for this kind of massive progressive policy output. Among the actions the *Times* called for were Medicare, tax reform, education reform, employment programs, antipoverty programs, housing and urban renewal, funding for mass transit and passenger railroads, pollution control, conservation, consumer protection, and an "overhaul" of Congress's rules and customs. "The voters have left the president and his party on Capitol Hill with no excuses," the *Times* concluded. "The time has come to make good on yesterday's brave promises and the bold statements of the ideal."[3]

The *Times* praised the president's aggressive efforts to move his Great Society agenda forward as well as his strategy of concealing his proposals and then presenting them dramatically in the State of the Union Address to avoid allowing an opposition movement to build. The key, it said, was to make the legislative process operate more efficiently.[4]

After the administration's first hundred-days, the *Washington Post* marveled at the congressional activism:

Congress has richly earned the praise that is being showered upon it. . . . If it keeps up the good work of the first 100 days, it will rank high among the most responsive Congresses of the present century.

This Congress has responded well to President Johnson's leadership. . . . Despite the powerful influence of President Johnson on Capitol Hill, there is far more give and take in the present executive-legislative relationship. To its great credit, the present Congress is legislating without resort to either the rubber stamp or blind obstructionism. It is giving the country . . . a fine example of representative government in action.[5]

Tom Wicker of the *Times* agreed and observed that "by the traditional Easter break most sessions of Congress have done little more than organize committees and hold hearings on a few bills," but the 89th Congress already had acted on far-reaching education, Medicare, voting-rights, poverty-aid, and presidential-succession measures. "The education and medicare bills alone would make most congressional sessions historic."[6]

Arthur Krock of the *Times* attributed the success of the hundred days to Johnson's leadership acumen and changes in Congress that led to a turnover in personnel and some key committee positions. Krock made clear that the legislative process worked best under the leadership of a strong president.[7]

A *Times* editorial added that the quickened pace of legislation was praiseworthy given the usual congressional bottleneck.[8] The *Times* assessed that the first days of the 89th Congress had shown how the policy process could work efficiently and effectively: "Now that Congress has begun to act as a creative partner with the Executive branch in the legislative enterprise, rather than merely a critic, obstructionist and irritant, there are few discernible limits to what it can achieve for the common good."9

Later in the year, when journalists reflected on the accomplishments of the session, enthusiasm had not subsided. James Reston wrote that "President Johnson is beginning to make Franklin Roosevelt's early legislative record look like an abject failure. He's getting everything through the Congress but the abolition of the Republican Party, and he hasn't tried that yet." Reston called LBJ's legislative record a "political miracle" and "a revolution in the binding of a hymn book. He has broken the consolidating spirit of the Eisenhower era." Reston credited in part the new Congress composed of freshman members committed to progressive reforms. Although many people had questioned the ability of our constitutional system to put forth policies to address social and economic problems, the 89th Congress had disproved these doubts. "This is a development of worldwide significance."10

Tom Wicker, along with others, called the work of the 89th Congress "the most extensive record of legislative accomplishment since FDR's Hundred Days" and noted that "the presidency is still the paramount force in the American government, the Congress is neither an obstructionist anachronism nor a rubber stamp." Nonetheless, Congress had not "developed the sort of active, sustained and intelligent influence on national policy that ought to be its true role in the 20th century."11

A New York Times editorial suggested that the president should continue to take advantage of the opportunity because much more needed to be done, and Congress "has its own tempo and tends to work in spurts." The editorial concluded that "the 89th Congress is of that rare breed: it moves to a presidential tempo."12 An August Times editorial assessed that Congress's "outstanding record" merited all of the praise.13

William S. White reflected on the "unprecedented congressional actions" of the "extraordinary" session and marveled at what he called "the profound and unexampled scope of the legislation that has moved so sedately and surely through the Senate and House." He added, "What Congress under Mr. Johnson's spur is doing in all fields of social legislation is in depth and total meaning beyond what any Congress has ever done for any president in any like period—not excluding Franklin D. Roosevelt at the top of his power."14

When Congress adjourned in October, Marquis Childs wrote of the legislative session that "however it is judged, the score is as impressive as any in this century. New legislation has meant advances in every field from the arts to medical care to highway beautification. The program has been the president's, bearing his stamp to an extent unequaled since the Hundred

Days of the New Deal."[15] Drew Pearson reported, "I have watched every president since Warren Harding and no Congress in that time achieved a record equal to the 89th Congress." He attributed much of this success to the many progressive, reform-minded Democratic legislators who "put new verve into the tired old seniors who had been around so long that their idealism was tarnished, their ambition jaded." Pearson concluded that the new Congress, working under LBJ's able leadership, had produced unprecedented policies.[16] Rowland Evans and Robert Novak agreed that the session would "go down in history as perhaps the most productive ever, with President Johnson winning passage of landmark legislation that had been bottled up for years."[17] Tom Wicker also praised the activist Congress as "one of the most remarkable of this century." He continued, "Congress proved itself neither a rubber stamp nor a balky mule. Mr. Johnson showed himself a shrewd, powerful leader rather than a magician, and those who had begun to regard Congress as a dragging anchor on the executive were given a fresh perspective on its potentiality."[18]

The *Washington Post* commented that Congress had acted to fulfill "the two profound impulses" of the Enlightenment. "One of these was the concept of the equality of man—and this session of Congress has done as much as any session since the Civil War to reaffirm that principle and to give it practical effect. The other was the notion that well doing is not the province of individual behavior alone but a purpose of government itself." The *Post* offered a "salute" to the president, Congress, and our democratic system: "It has been a great and heartening demonstration of the workability of our institutions in a time of rapid and almost revolutionary change. The president and the Congress together have written a great record of achievement."[19]

The *New York Times* boldly declared that "the 89th Congress . . . has been the best Congress since World War II." The *Times* extolled the "general excellence and comprehensiveness of this session's record," in contrast to past legislative sessions that had made Congress "the object of severe but justified public criticism." The *Times* noted that such criticism was justified due to Congress's long-standing inability to enact far-reaching, imaginative policies to solve social and economic problems.

The Congress elected a year ago broke the mold. A new majority coalition of Democrats and liberal Republicans has emerged. The seniority system remained, but the House rules were modified in a modest way that helped ease the flow of legislation to the floor. Rather than making a virtue out of sulky obstinacy, this Congress has cooperated with the executive branch to shape a constructive program. . . .

At last the decks have been cleared of numerous old problems and old quarrels. At last the nation has had the benefit of the work of a modern-minded Congress that addressed itself to the needs of a complicated industrial society entering the last third of the twentieth century.[20]

A *Times* news summary iterated the point:

[LBJ] has every reason to sing the praises of the 89th. It has approved, substantially intact, a legislative program containing—in the liberal and old-fashioned sense of the word—revolutionary proposals. The seminal acts in that program . . . may be expected to revolutionize profoundly the lives of American citizens and the quality of the national life.[21]

Despite these praises, some press commentaries noted Congress's failure to enact other far-reaching programs. Congress rejected LBJ's proposals for rent subsidies, a national teacher corps, home rule for the District of Columbia, repeal of section 14(b) of the Taft-Hartley Act authorizing right-to-work laws, and strict ethics codes. The *Times* praised the Congress's "distinguished display of legislative productivity" and "exhilarating record" but nevertheless noted that these failures pointed to the "glaring defects" of the session. The *Times* believed that the 89th Congress was praiseworthy, but an even more activist Congress would have been better.[22]

The *Wall Street Journal* did not concur with "the deluge of praise." Congress, it warned, had embarked upon a "flood of thoughtless, inflation-threatening legislation." Recalling the *New York Times* characterization of the 89th Congress as "the best since World War II," as well as other praises, the *Journal* demurred:

That's lavish acclaim indeed for an institution which, in the not too distant past, was being roundly condemned for its lethargy, its unresponsiveness to the needs of the nation. How has Congress accomplished the transition from brickbats to bouquets? Certainly the lawmakers have passed lots of legislation . . . [and] laid out lots of the taxpayers' money. . . . It's not at all clear, however, that all of the laws and all of the spending will help meet the country's real requirements.[23]

Raymond Moley also expressed reservations about the pace of the legislative process. "Very few members of Congress had the slightest idea how these beneficial gestures were going to be realized. They merely voted for the bills and dumped the job of management upon an already overburdened bureaucracy. . . . Good intentions alone will never create a great society."[24]

The enormous legislative activity overwhelmed other events in Congress that otherwise would have received more coverage. The session opened with important reforms that paved the way for policy activism. These included changing a rule to allow a majority of the House to vote to dislodge bills that had been waiting for clearance by the Rules Committee for at least twenty-one days; a change to allow the House by majority vote to send a bill to conference with the Senate, ending the practice of permitting the objection of a single member to send a bill back to the Rules Committee; and elimination of a rule that allowed a single member to block a vote for a day by requesting a printed copy of the legislation. The *Washington Post* praised these as "a splendid start" but noted the need for further reforms to "strike at the blind workings of the seniority system." In reiteration of its stance twenty years before, it called for "an overall study of the rules of Congress, along the lines of the La Follette–Monroney study in 1946. Such a study could well ask why it is that Congress is the only democratic legislature in the world that hews solely to seniority in naming powerful committee chairmen."[25] The *New York Times* also praised the House reforms, which had been required for "putting its own affairs in order. Ultimately, it stopped short of instituting a revision of its irresponsible seniority system. . . . The need to curb seniority is as plain as ever."[26] To the extent that the press noticed congressional reform in 1965, coverage emphasized the need for more reforms to make the legislative process efficient. Nonetheless, the hectic pace of legislation had somewhat "stilled the clamor for congressional reform."[27]

Still, Congress received high press marks for its performance. Journalists applauded its policy activism and reform; they held slow decisionmaking and tradition in low esteem. Congress's performance in 1965 may represent the press's ideal of how the legislative branch should operate. Although Congress is not geared toward efficient operation, journalists believed that it needed to improve its efficiency. To the extent that the press criticized the 89th Congress, 1st session, with the exception of the *Wall Street Journal*, it did so for not moving more aggressively in domestic policy and for not enacting sweeping internal reforms.

HOUSE AND SENATE ETHICS CODES (1968)

In 1968, when Congress took up the problem of member violations of ethical conduct, concern inside and outside the institution had long been building over such matters as the sources and uses of campaign funds and conflicts of interest. Some members had been able to make substantial incomes from private business interests and law practices while serving in Congress. Some even had financial holdings in industries regulated by the government. But although members had been disciplined from time to time for unethical or dishonest behavior, it was not until scandals dramatized breaches of ethical conduct that matters of behavior began to come under sustained scrutiny and the reform of ethics codes was pushed to the fore of the legislative agenda.

The instigation occurred in 1963, when Bobby Baker, secretary of the Senate majority, was charged with using his position to promote private financial interests. In 1964, the Senate established the bipartisan six-member Select Committee on Standards and Conduct. It was granted the authority to investigate Senate members and staff charged with improper behavior. The committee's first investigation resulted in the 1967 Senate censure of Senator Thomas J. Dodd of Connecticut for improper use of campaign contributions.

In the House, investigations into numerous improprieties on the part of Representative Adam Clayton Powell of New York also publicized the need for stronger oversight of members' ethical conduct. In 1967, the House established its bipartisan twelve-member Committee on Standards of Official Conduct. In 1968, the House and Senate committees proposed a number of reforms for the codes of ethics of their respective chambers.

On March 22, 1968, by a 67–1 vote, the Senate adopted the recommendations of the Senate committee to limit the outside employment of Senate employees, provide for disclosure of gifts of more than $50 and honoraria more than $300, and require all senators, their employees, and senatorial candidates earning $15,000 a year or more to file sealed financial reports with the U.S. comptroller general. The Senate rejected a proposal for full public disclosure of member finances. The House also adopted ethics rules, including Rule 43, which, among other requirements, prohibited the use of official position to receive compensation and acceptance of gifts from people with an interest in pending legislation. It also limited honoraria and prohibited personal use of campaign funds. The House also adopted Rule 44, requiring members and certain staff to file reports on their financial interests with the House Committee on Standards of Official Conduct.

Press coverage of the ethics-reform efforts was generally unfavorable. Although the House and Senate had taken important steps to strengthen their codes of conduct, editorialists emphasized what Congress did not do. The *Washington Post* declared that the "reports of the Senate and the House Committees on Ethics leave much to be desired" and described the Senate committee's recommendations as "a net gain, but a narrow and disappointing one." The *Post* found the somewhat broader House committee recommendations merely "a useful beginning." The editorial criticized the Senate's failure to require full public disclosure of members' financial interests: "Reports held in confidential files can be of little value in policing day-to-day conflicts of interest."[28] A week later, another editorial stated that "the Senate's desires for a code of ethics greatly outran its willingness to be restrained by the ethical rules." It described the Senate as "very eager indeed to improve its image," but not serious enough to have adopted far-reaching reforms, and characterized the Senate effort as a "first feeble effort" with an outcome that "was far from being satisfactory."[29] Still, it added, "the courageous advocates of a stricter code should find it easier to patch up the holes in the new framework than to start from scratch."[30]

The *New York Times* stated, "Since Congress has been notoriously and deliberately obtuse on the subject of ethical standards, the reports submitted to both houses last week have to be considered progress. But the report to the House is less than ideal, and the Senate committee's 'important beginning' is hopelessly inadequate." The *Times* deplored the failures to require full financial disclosure and to eliminate testimonial dinners.[31] A second editorial called the Senate code a "most unsatisfactory document, pretentious in aim and pathetic in fulfillment. . . . In short, the committee came up with the kind of ethical code that a corrupt man could easily live by—presuming he had intelligence and a little tact." The *Times* concluded that "the job of writing a comprehensive and effective ethics code remains to be done all over again."[32] After Senate adoption of the committee rules, the *Times* managed to offer faint praise—"some ethics are better than no ethics"—but it still deplored the failure to accept full public disclosure of business interests and earnings.[33]

The *Wall Street Journal* declared of the Senate's 67–1 vote to adopt the committee proposals that "only Senator George Aiken had the courage to label the code as 'the farce of the year.' " Although the *Journal* said that the proposed House and Senate codes were marginal improvements, the editorial concluded that Congress "should have done a better job of setting standards."[34] In an op-ed column, *Journal* writer Jerry Landauer summed up the mood: "Congress, quick to pounce on indiscretions elsewhere and more scarred by scandal than the other two branches of government, is most reluctant to accept similar restrictions."[35]

A *Time* magazine news story joined the chorus, calling the Senate effort "a pale cautionary code unlikely to infringe on the rules of the club or invade any Senator's privacy." *Time* portrayed the Senate effort as an attempt to protect an old club's outmoded practices:

> Behind a thicket of perquisites and protocol, the U.S. Senate has long guarded its majesty from the vulgar eye. It forbids cameras in the visitors' galleries, permits a member to edit gaucheries and gaffes out of his speeches before they appear in the *Congressional Record*, grants Senators a unique immunity from legal action for what they say in committee or on the floor.[36]

Like legislative reorganization, however, ethics reforms received little press attention. Although coverage of the controversies surrounding Baker, Dodd, and Powell had been heavy, institutional efforts to prevent recurrences lacked the immediate human appeal. This disjuncture lends credibility to the belief widely held among media scholars that the press gives much greater emphasis to stories involving personal controversy, rivalry, and scandal than it does to ones dealing with complex policy issues and institutional processes.

THE LEGISLATIVE REORGANIZATION ACT (1970)

The Legislative Reorganization Act of 1970 (P.L. 91–510) was the first such law for reforming Congress since 1946 and the first in a series of major reforms of Congress adopted in the 1970s. The reforms have profoundly influenced the nature of the legislative process.

Although the 1970 act had its origins in a 1966 reorganization bill that failed to pass the House Rules Committee in 1968, it did not go as far as the earlier defeated proposal. It did not fully address the problems of the seniority system, nor did it attempt to limit the power of the House Rules Committee and the Senate cloture rule. The law did, however, open Congress up to closer public scrutiny. Committee roll-call votes now had to be made public. The House practice of voting in anonymity by unrecorded teller votes was abolished. Prior to the new law, individual members' votes were not recorded, allowing the members to avoid accountability. Furthermore, the act also decreed that committees must have written rules, a reaction against the arbitrary power of some committee chairmen.

Certain rules affected only the Senate. For example, minority-party members of a committee could now call witnesses at hearings. A majority of committee members could call meetings in spite of a chairman's refusal to do so. A senator was limited to membership on two major committees and one minor, select, or joint committee. No member could serve on more than one of the more powerful committees—Armed Services, Appropriations, Finance, and Foreign Relations—and no member could chair more than one full committee and one subcommittee of a major committee.

As with the 1968 ethics reforms, to the partisans of fundamental change, the 1970 act represented, at best, a useful first step. The press also perceived the legislative reorganization effort as a step in the right direction, but not far-reaching enough. *New York Times* editorial board member Robert Bendiner wrote that "Congress as an institution has failed over a long span of years to change in the least degree with the times. In its organization, its division into feudal baronies, its veneration of procedures which are neither democratic nor efficient, it is in fact running a grave risk of becoming no more than a negative check on the executive branch or perhaps a captious subordinate of the judiciary." Bendiner harshly criticized the failure to reform the seniority system and concluded that members must have been satisfied with "the whole cozy arrangement because it guarantees them, if they are cooperative, the power to favor their constituents."[37]

Most of the press, however, welcomed even limited efforts to reform legislative rules and seniority. The *Wall Street Journal* editorialized that "there must be a better way. There are definite drawbacks to a system that fails to give adequate recognition and responsibility to younger members' talents and ambitions."[38] In response to a Democratic caucus decision in March 1970 to allow the Democratic Study Group to examine the seniority system, the *New York Times* commented, "Revolutions in the House of Representatives are so rare that even the limited concession won by Democrats opposed to the seniority system must be considered an important advance." But the *Times* was disappointed that Congress failed to move boldly and quickly to rid the institution of "this sixty-year old blight."[39] In July, after a preliminary decision by the House to eliminate the practice of not recording teller votes, the *Times* praised the decision. "Those who were not quite convinced by the moon landings that this is an era of change should be persuaded by the recent behavior of the House of Representatives." The *Times* lamented the price of acceptance of this reform: the decision of the House not to address "that fundamental evil," the seniority system.[40] *Times* reporter William V. Shannon also wrote that the House had taken a positive, though incomplete, step:

The House of Representatives, which is supposed to be the part of the federal government closest to the people, has long hidden many of its significant operations behind a bewildering set of procedures. Most members preferred it that way and the public did not seem to care. It was therefore a major shift in the House's sense of itself when it decided last week to abandon the most important of these procedures, the unrecorded teller vote. . . . The abolition of teller votes still left the House of Representatives far short of becoming a completely open and fully accountable body.

Shannon also lamented the failure of the House to reform the seniority system and to open committee meetings to full public view.[41]

After passage of the House bill in September, the *New York Times* declared that the chamber had "made progress in opening up its procedures to public scrutiny." The *Times* criticized the lack of a more far-reaching reform effort: "Every reform which opens up the House and democratizes its procedures makes it that much more responsive to public opinion. But the bill has a grave defect because it does not touch the least democratic feature of congressional life, the seniority system. . . . Incomplete though it is, this bill is certainly better than no bill."[42]

The *Washington Post* also praised the decision to end unrecorded teller voting. "The right of a free people to know how their elected representatives vote is a right without which elections can be considered neither free nor meaningful."[43] The *Post* also described the congressional reforms as inadequate:

Unfortunately, the House knocked out a provision requiring all committee meetings to be open to the public unless closed by majority vote. . . . Congress should not be allowed to forget that the major sources of its inefficiency and loss of public confidence remain untouched. Nothing in the bill would alter the elevation of misfits into key positions through the seniority system. Nor did the House take advantage of the occasion to give its leadership power to make and carry out an agenda. . . . So the great tasks of congressional reform still lie ahead.[44]

After the November midterm elections, the *New York Times* observed that the House would hardly be changed at all by a turnover of only fifty members and, more important, because of the entrenched seniority system that "guarantees that the House system of power will remain sluggish." Furthermore,

A major overhaul has long been needed in both chambers of Congress, but particularly in the House. It is the rigid observance of seniority that stultifies and obstructs the work of the House. It is seniority that makes the House a graveyard of talent and drives able, younger members to run for other office. . . . The legislative branch of the government cannot be responsive to the public unless the majority party assumes the responsibility to act. The seniority system defeats responsible government because it gives excessive scope to special-interest groups, parochial pressures and personal aggrandizement.[45]

The editor of *U.S. News and World Report*, David Lawrence, similarly wrote that "after 18 decades . . . we do not have a responsible system of government and . . . divisiveness inside the governmental structure impairs the efficiency of its operations." Lawrence also blamed the seniority system, as well as the system of staggered elections, which "discourages any sense of responsibility."[46]

Finally, a *Newsweek* report, "Congress's Nine Old Men," examined the "inefficient, undemocratic and largely unfunctioning parliamentary machinery" that inspired the calls for reform. It identified nine committee chairmen, all older than age seventy, who held enormous power. The report labeled four of them as "fighting," "traveling," "ailing," and "forgetting," whereas the other five were "not necessarily the best, but simply the longest-lived." The article concluded that "despite all the reformist oratory, the Nine Old Men seem as snug in their chairmanships as Abraham Lincoln's statue does in its marble mausoleum down by the Potomac."[47]

Press commentary on the 1970 legislative reform efforts was thus strikingly uniform. Congress was a bastion of outdated traditions that impeded change, openness, procedural democracy, and even realization of the values of the young. None of the editorials, op-eds, or news commentaries defended seniority. They applauded efforts to improve openness and procedural democracy. For the press, the more sweeping the reform proposal, the better. The major criticism was that Congress did not enact the most fundamental reforms proposed by liberal activists.

THE WATERGATE INVESTIGATION/CONGRESSIONAL REFORMS (1973–1974)

As the Watergate scandal unfolded over nearly two years, Congress took the lead in exposing the various crimes and improprieties committed in the Nixon White House. At no other time in history had Congress so dramatically and effectively exercised its duty as the "grand inquest of the nation." As the Senate Select Committee on Watergate, chaired by Senator Sam Ervin (D–N.C.), and the House Judiciary Committee, chaired by Representative Peter Rodino (D–N.J.), conducted public hearings on the coverup, Congress came under the watchful eyes of the nation. Reporters carefully evaluated Congress's performance, and their commentaries tell much about the qualities they found praiseworthy in the nation's legislature and those they deplored.

Not surprisingly, Watergate press coverage focused on the revelations of executive-branch wrongdoing and on the drama that resulted in the downfall of the Nixon presidency. But when the press did focus on Congress, its portrait was generally flattering, the portrait of an institution that dispatched enormous responsibilities effectively during a constitutional crisis.

January 1973–June 1973

Although some partisans criticized Congress early in the investigations for disrupting the nation's policy agenda, the press encouraged the legislature to assume the responsibilities of the nation's grand inquest. The *Washington Post* called the Ervin committee hearings "an undertaking of enormous importance to the mechanisms by which we try to maintain our freedom." It added that "there is a large public interest to be served in finding out all there is to know about the whole affair" and that a congressional inquiry, not a criminal trial, offered the best opportunity to achieve that end.[48] The *New York Times* noted that Congress had the duty to find the truth, assess the damage, and pass laws to correct the weaknesses of the governing system. It called on Congress to enact campaign-finance reforms to end the "corrupting flow of money."[49]

Many commentators extolled the benefits from a newly resurgent Congress. Vermont Royster of the *Wall Street Journal* wrote that despite all the criticism of its lack of independence from the presidency, credit belonged to Congress for preventing the Watergate affair "from being buried."[50] James M. Naughton of the *New York Times* wrote that "the White House is slipping and Congress is rising as the balance of power in Washington is being altered perceptibly by the Watergate conspiracy case." He added that Congress, "long a slumbering giant," had awakened to challenge the president's authority.[51] The *New York Times* observed:

> While the Executive slips into deeper disarray, a rejuvenated Congress has begun to move with remarkable determination and unity of

purpose to restore the balance of power that the Founding Fathers had perceptively prescribed to check excesses of any branch of the Federal Government. . . . The revival of the constitutional system of checks and balances through an awakened Congress offers hope for ultimate restoration of the nation's damaged political health.[52]

The *Times* subsequently offered editorials that praised the investigation. The newspaper extolled the "educative function" of the Ervin committee.[53] Despite administration claims that the inquiries diverted congressional attention from urgent national issues, the *Times* defended the "essential work" of the committee[54] and declared that "no other item of public business is more important. . . . No other forum is more appropriate—indeed, no other forum is available—for this inquest."[55]

Nonetheless, press comments were not wholly laudatory. The *Times* expressed concern that Watergate had diverted congressional attention from "disastrous cuts" in administration spending on social programs and regretted that Congress lacked the internal machinery required to assess national budgetary needs. It advised Congress to adopt reforms to challenge administration budget analyses.[56] The *Washington Post* criticized Congress for allowing the president to impound funds for programs enacted by the legislature. Constitutional processes would be subverted, it said, if Congress failed to assert its power over federal spending.[57] Other press commentaries also emphasized the need for the legislature to become more aggressive in asserting its prerogatives.[58]

During the early stages of the hearings, the Nixon White House complained that the Ervin committee was taking too long and not accomplishing much. Press commentaries replied that the hearings were too crucial to be hurried along.[59] When Special Prosecutor Archibald Cox expressed concern that the hearings could prejudice the legal process, the *Washington Post* responded that the Senate had to continue the hearings to help the nation get through the crisis.[60] Even the *Wall Street Journal*, which had been critical of the effects of the hearings on the presidency, declared that the Ervin committee "may be the last best hope for restoring public confidence in American political processes."[61] In a later editorial, the *Journal* hinted at the need for reforms to strengthen Congress's policymaking role in the event of a post-Watergate weakened presidency. It cited the familiar criticisms of Congress as generally being incapable of decisive decisionmaking and concluded, "It will not be easy for Congress, as it is now organized, to assume a greater leadership role even if the presidency loses some of its influence."[62]

July 1973–December 1973

In attempting to sway public opinion against continued Watergate hearings, President Nixon persisted in maintaining that Congress was "wallowing in Watergate" while the nation's business went unattended. Nixon's defenders warned that the public hearings weakened the country's stature abroad.

The press defended Congress and continued to urge it to persist. "Watergate, far from slowing the Congress down," the *Washington Post* commented, "has actually spurred it to great activity and independence. This may be little comfort to the president, but it should be welcome news for a nation which—*before* Watergate—probably had more reason to worry about weakness and inertia on Capitol Hill."[63]

The *New York Times* referred to pressures to end the hearings quickly as "partisan and self-serving." The hearings constituted "as grave a duty to discharge as any congressional committee [has had] in the history of the Republic," and besides, the record showed that "as many bills have been considered and voted upon as in the past sessions."[64] The *Times* later emphasized the imperative of the inquiries because "the judicial process alone cannot present to the nation a cohesive picture of the policies which came dangerously close to subverting free government." Furthermore, Congress had the responsibility to "transmit to the American people the knowledge that is essential to the reaffirmation of democratic rule."[65] Finally, it said that the

> Senate Watergate Committee had acted in the public interest by resisting political pressure to call off its hearings, or to close them to coverage by press and television. . . . Far from exposing the United States to criticism and ridicule, full public scrutiny of grievous violations of the public trust is reassuring to those, here and abroad, who cling to belief in the continued validity of government by the people.[66]

After the notorious Saturday Night Massacre, the *Times* implored Congress to continue the investigations and "to enable the courts and the grand jury to reconstitute the abolished office of special prosecutor." Congress, it said, had the highest duty to take action to ensure the independence of the special prosecutor.[67]

Clayton Fritchey called Nixon's accusation that Congress neglected important duties because of Watergate "without foundation." To Nixon's assertion, Fritchey responded that the Congress had in fact maintained a "fast pace" of legislative activity "by any standard" and praised the Watergate inquiries for their lasting contributions "to the commonweal."[68]

Newsweek also replied to Nixon's accusations by summarizing the accomplishments of the 93d Congress with high praises:

> As Congress closed its first session . . . its members had put in nearly 2,000 hours in debate, racked up a new record for roll-call votes—and enacted a staggering total of more than 200 new laws. . . . In foreign affairs, the Congress reaffirmed its policymaking role by forcing an end to U.S. bombing in Cambodia and by putting sharp new limits on the president's war-making powers. . . . The legislators moved to streamline their own budgeting procedures, and the House took a major step toward internal reform by limiting the role seniority plays in the choice of committee chairmen.[69]

Press coverage generally emphasized the need for Congress to reform the legislative process and curb presidential powers, and the press criticized Congress when it appeared not to be moving aggressively enough to enact reforms. A *New York Times* editorial chided the Senate Rules Committee for having tried to weaken campaign-finance reporting laws at a time when the Watergate scandal had "transformed the political scene."[70] The *Times* also proposed legislation to establish a truly independent and powerful office of special prosecutor.[71] But at the conclusion of the 1973 legislative session, the paper praised congressional challenges to presidential authority: "This 93rd Congress had destroyed President Nixon's hegemony and forcefully asserted its own authority. The initiative has passed from the White House to Capitol Hill. Historians may some day mark the decline of what one of them has called 'the Imperial Presidency' from Nov. 7, 1973, when Congress enacted the War Powers bill into law over Mr. Nixon's veto."[72]

James Reston also called for legislative reforms and extolled the need for "corrective legislation" to create "a more equal and corruption-proof system of paying for political campaigns." He regretted that campaign-finance reforms, although of enormous importance, rarely received news-media coverage.[73] The *Wall Street Journal*, although at times defending Nixon against Watergate charges, agreed that reforms were needed to curb presidential powers: "Liberals and conservatives alike agree that they have an obligation to curb presidential power and restore checks-and-balances." Furthermore, "This shift to congressional reassertion suggests a welcome end to the old era of an innocent belief in presidential omniscience."[74]

In October 1973, the House commenced a formal impeachment inquiry by the Committee on the Judiciary, chaired by Representative Peter W. Rodino (D–N.J.). The *New York Times* applauded the move. "In a way, it is a sign of constitutional health that the overlay of awe and fear covering the process of impeachment has been swept aside. . . . The Congress and its leaders would be no more justified in backing away from this provision of the Constitution than the president is in ignoring and defying other sections of the fundamental law of the Republic."[75]

Many journalists initially doubted whether Congress could carry out this extraordinary duty. Anthony Lewis wondered if Congress had determination enough to pursue impeachment or whether it would "go back to its usual ways of indecision and nest-feathering." Lewis argued that if it failed to move aggressively on the process of impeachment, "Congress would be known to have failed its ultimate constitutional duty."[76] William Raspberry charged that "Congress hasn't the guts to do its job" and that there was "no leadership in the House of Representatives." Members "only respond to polls and constituent pressures and generally do not carry out their constitutional responsibilities with distinction."[77] The *Wall Street Journal* also expressed a skeptical view. "Congress has assumed the duty of assuring the public that justice is done in the Watergate affair. It is a heavy burden for a body that shows all the weaknesses of any other committee of 535 souls. . . . It is the habit of Congress, as of other committees, to avoid difficult decisions, whenever possible."[78]

George Will maintained that after months of indecisiveness, "the intellectual seriousness of Mr. Nixon's construing of the Constitution deserves the definitive ruling that only the Congress can provide."[79] The *New York Times* again insisted that Congress enact legislation to ensure an independent special prosecutor and criticized the Rodino committee for failing to act."[80]

David Broder wrote one of the most critical commentaries on Congress's failure to move quickly on impeachment. Despite the weight of evidence, Congress's hesitation proved that "an opposition-controlled legislature is peculiarly ineffective in remedying or rectifying a serious abuse of power by the executive, even after it has occurred." Broder believed that members of Congress prolonged the controversy because they benefited politically. He criticized Congress for not enacting more stringent curbs on presidential powers.[81]

January 1974–June 1974

The press continued to praise Congress for undertaking the Watergate inquiries and for attempting to restore balance to the executive-legislative relationship. The *New York Times* praised the Ervin committee for educating the public and commented, "The nation owes a debt of gratitude to Senator Ervin and his colleagues for the delicate work they performed so tirelessly, for the impact and the impetus which they provided toward the task of awakening the national conscience."[82] David E. Rosenbaum agreed that "the committee's most lasting achievements were the civics lessons that it taught the American people and the detailed documentary record that it developed and passed on to the prosecutors and the impeachment inquiry." Another benefit was that "it almost certainly paved the way for more use of the investigative powers of Congress."[83]

After the House voted 410–4 to support an impeachment inquiry, the *New York Times* beamed that "such a demonstration of near-unanimity in this matter of grave national concern shows that members of both parties are deeply conscious of their constitutional responsibility to determine whether or not the manner in which the president has conducted himself constitutes cause for impeachment. . . . The clear-cut action by the House . . . signals an end to temporizing."[84] The paper later praised the Rodino committee for its "commendable and scrupulous concern for the integrity of the process to impeach President Nixon."[85]

Despite this praise, public esteem remained very low. A February 1973 Harris poll had shown that despite the efforts to resolve the national crisis, Congress had an even lower public approval rating than President Nixon (21 percent for Congress, 30 percent for Nixon). William S. White expressed surprise at these results because Congress had nothing to do with instigating Watergate, and he noted the irony that public anger was "directed primarily toward the Senate, which until lately has been the only active congressional show in town on Watergate, and specifically at the Senate Watergate committee." He considered Congress's actions praiseworthy, even if the public, at that stage of the crisis, did not agree.[86]

The press continued to applaud efforts to strengthen the legislature and weaken presidential powers. *Time* commended the "reappraisal of what the proper constitutional balance between the Executive and Legislative branches of Government should be."[87] Tom Wicker wrote that Congress needed to scrutinize and limit the powers of the presidency.[88] The *New York Times* editorialized that "with the Watergate scandals ravaging public confidence in the nation's political system, it would be reckless for the leadership of either party to frustrate the demand for reform."[89] *Newsweek* declared that Congress's post-Watergate task was "restoring the balance of power between [it] and the executive branch," if it did not lack the will to assert itself.[90]

Finally, Russell Baker criticized Congress for not having "considered itself in the imperial weight class with presidents." He characterized it as satisfied with conferring vast powers on the presidency while focusing its own energies on constituent service activities. Baker preferred an activist Congress willing to challenge presidential powers.[91]

By mid-1974, the press began once again to criticize Congress for not having moved quickly enough on impeachment. *Newsweek* called the Rodino committee "the tortoise on the Hill,"[92] and the *Washington Post* implored it to stop prolonging the inquiries in the hope that perhaps it could "avoid the burden of judgment."[93] Joseph Kraft asked, "How many times does the president have to streak before the Congress says he has no clothes?"[94] Joseph Alsop warned that the "entire U.S. government" would become paralyzed by "Watergate-Mania."[95] *Washington Post* editorial-page writer J. W. Anderson also cited the need for the Rodino committee "to step up the pace." He concluded that it was unhealthful for the country to have its president under a cloud of suspicion for too long. He believed that Congress could better serve the country by moving quickly on the issue of impeachment.[96]

July 1974–December 1974

As the Watergate crisis spiraled toward its conclusion, the press reflected favorably on the role Congress had played. The Rodino committee in particular was congratulated for its fairness in handling the impeachment inquiry, an assignment that the *New York Times* said "had few modern precedents or guidelines. . . . The country can rightly feel that a thorough, conscientious and nonpartisan job has been done."[97] The *Times* noted that despite concerns raised "that the members of Congress might disgrace themselves by prattling inanities before the cameras or by grandstanding," the Rodino committee instead offered "a display of which the committee can be proud and which the House and Senate—if it comes to that—should strive to match."[98] The *Times* offered additional congratulations to the committee in two other editorials:

Members of the House Judiciary Committee have been eloquent in conveying their sense of agony and awe at the decisions which chance has called upon them to make this summer of 1974. Less evident, but equally justified, is the sense of confidence among legislators and the observing public alike over the way this solemn and fateful political process is operating within the democratic structure. . . . The grueling ordeal through which the American political system has already been dragged is leading to an expression of its ultimate strength.[99]

The burden now moves to the entire House. If the debates there sustain the high level and dignified tone set by most of the members of the Judiciary Committee, the nation can look forward with confidence to the further working out of its constitutional processes for the restoration of legitimacy in the highest executive office.[100]

Times reporter William V. Shannon wrote that the Rodino committee hearings had refuted claims that the inquiries would tear apart the country. Instead, "The members of the committee have shown themselves to be conscientious and sensible. . . . Americans are gaining some encouragement by watching their elected representatives at work. They see them acting the way men and women ought to act in the political order." Also,

The debate is spirited but free of rancor, informed by intelligence, shaped by self-discipline and occasionally graced by eloquence. On both sides of the impeachment question, members are acting with dignity and responsibility. They are not selling their votes to the highest bidder, they are not trying to shout one another down, they are not throwing inkwells at one another, and no one is hammering the desk with his shoe. In short, in response to the threat of illegitimate power, a recurrent theme in human history, they are proving once again that the highly civilized and always difficult practice of self-government is possible.[101]

Anthony Lewis agreed and declared that "the system is working" and "Congress is facing the heaviest of responsibilities without flinching." Furthermore, the Rodino committee's hearings had "demonstrated that ordinary men and women can rise to a great occasion—can be trusted with the fate of a great country." He concluded that the Watergate hearings had restored "belief in our political process, and especially in the legislative branch of government."[102]

Times reporter R. W. Apple, Jr., wrote that the Rodino committee's hearings "were marked by a dignity commensurate with the occasion." As a result of the hearings, "Suddenly, the House is seen and sees itself as an institution worthy of respect."[103] The *Washington Post* summarized the significance of the proceedings:

The proceedings of the House Judiciary Committee have set an elevated and distinguished standard of judgment for all that must now follow. The Committee's debate has served to illuminate for the whole country the nature of political responsibility as Americans have traditionally understood it. The Committee has concentrated on the most important charges, and it has drawn them up in terms that ground them directly on the Constitution. In the Committee's debates, the opposition to impeachment has been carried on at a considerably higher level than any defense that the White House has ever provided for itself over these past two years. . . . The idea that all of American politics had fallen into decay has been demonstrated to be manifestly wrong. One element of our government went grievously astray, and now Congress is carefully proceeding to correct these errors.[104]

After Nixon's resignation, Congress turned to the reforms that had been called for. By the end of the legislative session, it had produced the War Powers Act, campaign-finance reform, creation of a joint congressional budget committee, a budget-control law, energy legislation, education aid, and pension-funds standards. *Time* applauded the "monumental reform in the financing of presidential campaigns" and emphasized the importance of broad-based reforms of the legislative process.[105] "Even allowing for the members' preoccupation with Nixon and Watergate for much of its tenure, the 93rd Congress amassed a respectable record and left behind durable achievements."[106] *Time* concluded that the reformists in Congress had broken the "restraints of tradition," and "the results were astonishing. For the House, that glacially sluggish institution, it amounted to a revolution."[107] *U.S. News* agreed that the 93d Congress would "go down in history for its action on Watergate" and that its "record has been a surprise to many who had expected the Watergate affair to crowd legislation off the agenda this year."[108]

Press coverage of Congress's role in investigating the Watergate scandal indicates what journalists expect from the legislative branch. They believed that Congress was at its best when investigating the executive branch, exposing corruption, and taking forthright action to remedy defects in the governing process—an activist, reformist Congress that was willing to assert and even strengthen its own powers. When Congress appeared to be moving too slowly in the Watergate investigations or not aggressively enough to enact institutional reforms, journalists implored the members for action. During Watergate, Congress received favorable press coverage that showed its capacity for leadership in a crisis, when it conducted its constitutional duties with a minimum of partisanship and petty politicking, performed a vital democratic function by educating the public about government corruption and threats to our constitutional system, and acted strongly to restore balance to the separation-of-powers system.

NOTES

1. "Congress Meets the Test," *New York Times*, October 18, 1965, p. 34.

2. "A Salute," *Washington Post*, October 24, 1965, p. E6.

3. "The New Congress," *New York Times*, January 3, 1965, sec. 4, p. 8. See also "Congress Gets Under Way," *New York Times*, January 6, 1965, p. 38: "The prospect is for an unusually busy and productive session in both houses"; Tom Wicker, "Johnson and Congress," *New York Times*, February 7, 1965, sec. 4, p. 5: "The outlook is for a highly productive session." See also "LBJ and Congress: After a Fast Start, Harder Tests Ahead," *U.S. News and World Report*, March 1, 1965, pp. 52–53.

4. "Strong Start on Capitol Hill," *New York Times*, January 17, 1965, sec. 4, p. 12.

5. "The First 100 Days," *Washington Post*, April 16, 1965, p. A20. Another *Post* editorial praised "the remarkable achievements of the first three months" by Congress and called for even more legislative action to fulfill "the promise of the first 100 days." See "Formidable Task," *Washington Post*, April 25, 1965, p. E6.

6. Tom Wicker, "Johnson's 100 Days: Domestic Achievements in Legislation Compared with Period under Roosevelt," *New York Times*, April 15, 1965, p. 22.

7. Arthur Krock, "In the Nation: At Breakneck Speed," *New York Times*, April 11, 1965, sec. 4, p. 15. See also William V. Shannon, "All the Way with LBJ?" *New York Times*, April 12, 1965, p. 34; "Congress: Hundred-Days Mark," *Newsweek*, April 19, 1965, p. 26; "LBJ's '100 Days'—A Record Piling Up," *U.S. News and World Report*, April 26, 1965, pp. 41–46.

8. "Big Week for Congress," *New York Times*, April 11, 1965, sec. 4, p. 14.

9. "Congress: Second Phase," *New York Times*, April 26, 1965, p. 30.

10. James Reston, "Washington: The Quiet Revolution," *New York Times*, August 6, 1965, p. 26.

11. Tom Wicker, "LBJ and Congress: No Rubber Stamps on the Hill," *New York Times*, August 29, 1965, sec. 4, p. 13. See also Tom Wicker, "Politics: The Man Who Delivered the Goods," August 31, 1965, p. 32; "Johnson and Congress," *New York Times*, June 20, 1965, sec. 4, p. 2.

12. "The President and Congress," *New York Times*, July 11, 1965, sec. 4, p. 10. See also "Big Week in Congress," *New York Times*, August 1, 1965, sec. 4, p. 10.

13. "The Paradox of Congress," *New York Times*, August 16, 1965, p. 26.

14. William S. White, "Johnson Program," *Washington Post*, August 4, 1965, p. A18.

15. Marquis Childs, "How LBJ Branded the 89th Congress," *Washington Post*, October 18, 1965, p. A16.

16. Drew Pearson, "Laws by the Loaf: President's Bread Breaking and Freshman Idealism Made 89th Congress a Smasher," *Washington Post*, October 24, 1965, p. E7. See also Tom Wicker, "Winds of Change in the Senate," *New York Times Magazine*, September 12, 1965, pp. 52–53, 119–120, 124.

17. Rowland Evans and Robert Novak, "Inside Report . . . Grumbling on the Hill," *Washington Post*, October 4, 1965, p. A21. See also Roscoe Drummond, "Wrong Answer on 89th," *Washington Post*, October 24, 1965, p. E7.

18. Tom Wicker, "The Fruitful Session," *New York Times*, October 25, 1965, p. 41. Wicker noted that "an effective relationship does not always require Congress to put its own mark on legislation." Wicker added that LBJ moved an education aid bill through Congress unchanged, overcoming the usual debate and amending of legislation.

19. "A Salute," p. E6.

20. "Congress Meets the Test," p. 34.

21. "Exit Congress," *New York Times*, October 24, 1965, sec. 4, p. 1.

22. "On a Note of Triumph," *New York Times*, October 24, 1965, sec. 4, p. 10. See also "Congress Meets the Test" and "Exit Congress"; "Congress: Squaring Off over 14(b)," *Time*, October 1, 1965, p. 30; "When Congress Got Its Back Up," *U.S. News and World Report*, October 11, 1965, pp. 41–42.

23. "From Brickbats to Bouquets," *Wall Street Journal*, October 26, 1965, p. 16. See also "A Frenzy of Lawmaking," *Wall Street Journal*, August 4, 1965, p. 8: "There is indeed no good reason for the rush on Capitol Hill. The nation would be better off if the lawmakers could somehow pause and reflect on the totality of their effort, instead of turning out a mass of legislation in so hyperactive a state."

24. Raymond Moley, "Laws: Then What Next?" *Newsweek*, October 11, 1965, p. 116. See also Raymond Moley, "State-Local Finances," *Newsweek*, May 3, 1965, p. 100; Raymond Moley, "Tax Help for Parents," *Newsweek*, October 18, 1965, p. 132; Raymond Moley, "Inefficient Colleges," *Newsweek*, October 25, 1965, p. 124; Henry C. Wallich, "The Powerful Society," *Newsweek*, October 4, 1965, p. 84; Henry Hazlitt, "Great Society's Cost," *Newsweek*, November 22, 1965, p. 90; Walter Lippmann, "The Great—and Good—Society," *Newsweek*, November 22, 1965, p. 25; "Not by Popular Demand," *Wall Street Journal*, April 30, 1965, p. 16; "Restiveness on Capitol Hill," *Wall Street Journal*, July 2, 1965, p. 6; "Pause for Digestion," *Wall Street Journal*, October 4, 1965, p. 16.

25. "Housecleaning," *Washington Post*, January 5, 1965, p. A12. See also "Congress Looking Inward," *Washington Post*, May 12, 1965, p. A14.

26. "Congress Gets Under Way," p. 38.

27. William V. Shannon, "Congress: Reform Still Needed," *New York Times*, September 6, 1965, p. 14. See also Arthur Krock, "In the Nation: A Bureaucratic Explosion," *New York Times*, May 13, 1965, p. 36; Tom Wicker, "Congress: What Role in the Twentieth Century," *New York Times*, August 24, 1965, p. 30.

28. "Watchmen on the Hill," *Washington Post*, March 18, 1968, p. A16.

29. "Senatorial Code of Ethics," *Washington Post*, March 25, 1968, p. A14.

30. Ibid.

31. "Slow Start on Ethics," *New York Times*, March 20, 1968, p. 46.

32. "No Gain for Ethics," *New York Times*, March 24, 1968, sec. 4, p. 16.

33. "Senatorial Ethics," *New York Times*, November 28, 1968, p. 36.

34. "On Legislating Morality," *Wall Street Journal*, March 27, 1968, p. 16.

35. Jerry Landauer, "Myth of the Part-Time Congressman," *Wall Street Journal*, April 15, 1968, p. 18. See also Jerry Landauer, "Reforms to Prevent Another Dodd Scandal Urged by Ethics Unit; Senate Backing Seen," *Wall Street Journal*, March 18, 1968, p. 8; Jerry Landauer, "Quiet Burials for Congress Reforms," *Wall Street Journal*, September 6, 1968, p. 8.

36. "The Congress: Guarding the Assets," *Time*, March 29, 1968, p. 25. See also "Congress: Keeping Them Honest," *Newsweek*, April 15, 1968, p. 50.

37. Robert Bendiner, "Congress in the Age of Aquarius," *New York Times*, January 19, 1970, p. 46. See also "Who Will Abolish Seniority?" *Washington Post*, February 17, 1970, p. A14; "Spotlight on Seniority," *Washington Post*, March 24, 1970, p. A18; David Broder, "Revolt of Liberal Democrats in the House Is Long Overdue," *Washington Post*, March 24, 1970, p. A19.

38. "The Young Liberals' Problem," *Wall Street Journal*, February 26, 1970, p. 16. See also Tom Wicker, "In the Nation: Opening Up the House," *New York Times*, March 17, 1970, p. 42; "Uprising on Capitol Hill," *New York Times*, February 18, 1970, p. 46; John W. Finney, "Democrats in Congress See Need for a 'Revolution,' " *New York Times*, February 22, 1970, sec. 4, p. 1; "Alternatives to Seniority," *New York Times*, February 23, 1970, p. 26.

39. "Rebellion in the House," *New York Times*, March 22, 1970, sec. 4, p. 16. See also "Lights On in Congress," *New York Times*, July 22, 1970, p. 40.

40. "New Day on Capitol Hill," *New York Times*, July 29, 1970, p. 38.

41. William V. Shannon, "The House Decides to Stop Being So Secretive," *New York Times*, August 2, 1970, sec. 4, p. 3.

42. "Open House," *New York Times*, September 26, 1970, p. 28.

43. "Open House," *Washington Post*, July 29, 1970, p. A22.

44. "Down Payment on Congressional Reform," *Washington Post*, September 22, 1970, p. A20.

45. "Seniority under Attack," *New York Times*, November 18, 1970, p. 46. See also Marquis Childs, "New Ball Game for the House," *Washington Post*, November 18, 1970, p. A19.

46. David Lawrence, "Why Not Four Years for Both the President and Congress?" *U.S. News and World Report*, February 2, 1970, p. 76.

47. "Congress's Nine Old Men," *Newsweek*, February 2, 1970, pp. 20–21. See also John W. Finney, "Generation Gap in the House: The Young Want More Power," *New York Times*, March 22, 1970, sec. 4, p. 3; Tom Wicker, "Stamping Out Seniority," *New York Times*, December 8, 1970, p. 47.

48. "Watergate: The Trial and the Senate," *Washington Post*, January 15, 1973, p. A20.

49. "Senate Duty," *New York Times*, May 3, 1973, p. 42.

50. Vermont Royster, "Thinking Things Over," *Wall Street Journal*, May 8, 1973, p. 26.

51. James M. Naughton, "Congress Ascending," *New York Times*, May 12, 1973, pp. 1, 6.

52. "Congress Awakens," *New York Times*, May 20, 1973, sec. 4, p. 16.

53. "The Hearings Go On," *New York Times*, June 6, 1973, p. 46.

54. "Watergate Pressures," *New York Times*, June 2, 1973, p. 30.

55. "A Proper Forum," *New York Times*, June 15, 1973, p. 36.

56. "Neglected Agenda," *New York Times*, June 18, 1973, p. 28.

57. "The Impoundment Battle," *Washington Post*, February 6, 1973, p. A18.

58. See, for example, Alan L. Otten, "Whose Emergency?" *Wall Street Journal*, January 18, 1973, p. 12; Alan L. Otten, "Power Plays," *Wall Street Journal*, January 26, 1973, p. 12; Fred M. Hechinger, "Executive Obligation," *New York Times*, April 16, 1973, p. 37.

59. See, for example, Tom Wicker, "No Time To 'Get It Over With,' " *New York Times*, June 3, 1973, sec. 4, p. 17; Anthony Lewis, "Rush to Judgment," *New York Times*, June 4, 1973, p. 35; William Raspberry, "The Senate Hearings: 'Let Them Drone On,' " *Washington Post*, June 8, 1973, p. A29.

60. "Watergate: There Is No Quick or Easy Way Out," *Washington Post*, June 6, 1973, p. A18. See also "Two Investigations; Two Different Goals," *Washington Post*, May 17, 1973, p. A26.

61. "The Senate Hearings," *Wall Street Journal*, May 22, 1973, p. 26.

62. "Congress and the Presidency," *Wall Street Journal*, June 4, 1973, p. 16.

63. "Congress, the Hearings, and the Nation's Business," *Washington Post*, August 19, 1973, p. C6.

64. "No Undue Haste," *New York Times*, September 10, 1973, p. 34.

65. "The Committee's Task," *New York Times*, September 24, 1973, p. 32.

66. "The Hearings Continue," *New York Times*, September 13, 1973, p. 46.

67. "Congress Must Decide," *New York Times*, October 22, 1973, p. 30.

68. Clayton Fritchey, "The Unfinished Business," *Washington Post*, August 25, 1973, p. A17.

69. "Congress: The Do-Something 93rd," *Newsweek*, December 31, 1973, p. 12.

70. "Looking Backward," *New York Times*, July 11, 1973, p. 40.

71. "No Strings," *New York Times*, October 26, 1973, p. 42.

72. "Political Reversal," *New York Times*, December 23, 1973, sec. 4, p. 10.

73. James Reston, "Let's Hear from Congress," *New York Times*, November 30, 1973, p. 37.

74. "End of an Era," *Wall Street Journal*, October 23, 1973, p. 24.

75. "Impeachment," *New York Times*, October 31, 1973, p. 44.

76. Anthony Lewis, "Living with Illusion," *New York Times*, November 26, 1973, p. 31.

77. William Raspberry, "As Congress Drags Its Feet," *Washington Post*, December 5, 1973, p. A31.

78. "Congress's Burden," *Wall Street Journal*, November 19, 1973, p. 14.

79. George F. Will, "Impeachment for the Right Reason," *Washington Post*, October 23, 1973, p. A22. See also Joseph Kraft, "Forcing Mr. Nixon out of Office," *Washington Post*, October 23, 1973, p. A23: "There are many possible ways to achieve the one acceptable resolution of the present crisis—the forcing out of the president. The only real question is whether the country's leaders, especially in the House of Representatives, have the courage to be free men."

80. "Special Prosecutor," *New York Times*, November 2, 1973, p. 40.

81. David S. Broder, "Power: Theory and Reality," *Washington Post*, December 12, 1973, p. A30.

82. "Conscience Primer," *New York Times*, February 22, 1974, p. 32.

83. David E. Rosenbaum, "An Assessment of Ervin & Co.: Pathfinders," *New York Times*, April 28, 1974, sec. 4, p. 3.

84. "A United House," *New York Times*, February 7, 1974, p. 36.

85. "Fair Procedure," *New York Times*, May 4, 1974, p. 40.

86. William S. White, "The Decline of Congress," *Washington Post*, February 16, 1974, p. A19.

87. "Restoring the Federal Balance," *Time*, May 6, 1974, p. 14.

88. "The Man Is Not the Office," *New York Times*, March 17, 1974, sec. 4, p. 15.

89. "No Time for Delay," *New York Times*, April 23, 1974, p. 40.

90. "Checks and Balances," *Newsweek*, May 6, 1974, p. 76.

91. Russell Baker, "Moods of Washington," *New York Times Magazine*, March 24, 1974, pp. 71–72.

92. "The Tortoise on the Hill," *Newsweek*, June 10, 1974, pp. 23–25. An earlier critical news article is "Congress's Go-Slow Approach to the 'Nixon Problem,' " *U.S. News and World Report*, February 4, 1974, pp. 20–21.

93. "Protecting the Presidency," *Washington Post*, May 29, 1974, p. A18.

94. Joseph Kraft, "Impeachment: Toward a Decision on the Merits," *Washington Post*, June 2, 1974, p. C7.

95. Joseph Alsop, "The Impeachment Timetable," *Washington Post*, May 29, 1974, p. A19.

96. J. W. Anderson, "Impeachment Inquiry: Running Late," *Washington Post*, June 21, 1974, p. A22.

97. "Impeachable Offenses," *New York Times*, July 14, 1974, sec. 4, p. 16.

98. "A Sense of Duty," *New York Times*, July 26, 1974, p. 32.

99. "Agony and Pride," *New York Times*, July 30, 1974, p. 32.

100. "The Great Task Begun," *New York Times*, August 4, 1974, sec. 4, p. 16.

101. William V. Shannon, "The Arithmetic of Impeachment," *New York Times*, July 27, 1974, p. 29.

102. Anthony Lewis, "The People Do Govern," *New York Times*, July 29, 1974, p. 23.

103. R. W. Apple, Jr., "T.V. and Impeachment," *New York Times*, August 1, 1974, p. 13.

104. "The Judiciary Committee's Work," *Washington Post*, July 31, 1974, p. A20. The *Washington Post* criticized the Rodino committee on one count—failing to place more emphasis than it did in the articles of impeachment on the issue of political bribery and extortion in the case of American Milk Producers, Inc.,'s support of President Nixon. See also "Impeachment: ITT and Milk," *New York Times*, July 26, 1974, p. A26.

105. "Congress: Reforms for Others Only," *Time*, October 21, 1974, p. 38.

106. "Drawing Up a Balance Sheet on the 93rd," *Time*, December 23, 1974, p. 9.

107. "Congress: Return of King Caucus," *Time*, December 16, 1974, pp. 17–18.

108. "A Congress That Did a Lot Is Coming Back to Do More," *U.S. News and World Report*, November 4, 1974, pp. 33–34.

Chapter Four

The Era of Cynicism I
(1977–Early 1990s)

During the Era of Cynicism, congressional coverage became increasingly negative, often outright hostile. Much has been written of the corrosive impact of Watergate on the relationship between the press and political institutions. Most of the analyses focus on the negative coverage of the modern presidency. But in recent years, the degree of negative coverage of Congress has outpaced even that given to presidents. If Congress is the most reviled national institution, much of that state can be attributed to elite press coverage.

In part, as the following shows, Congress is victimized by inflated and often contradictory expectations. From the vantage of the press, Congress is both out of touch with the people it serves and too beholden to "special interests." Congress is expected to both challenge presidential authority and work with the chief executive to end gridlock. Members must project the highest standards of personal and professional conduct and be the most qualified people available to serve; yet they should not be paid too much. In the modern era, it seems, no matter what Congress does, people complain, and the elite press has been leading the charge against Congress in a fashion that appears to be shaking the very foundation of representative government.

THE PROSPECTS FOR PARTY GOVERNANCE (1977)

After the tumultuous Nixon years, the unprecedented reforms of Congress, and the 1976 election of Jimmy Carter to the White House, the country appeared poised for a new era in presidential-congressional relations. Eight years of divided government (Democratic Congress, Republican White House) had taken a toll on the country, and the prospects for activist government seemed favorable under one-party leadership of the federal government. A *New York Times* editorial after Carter's election expressed a common view: "The election of Jimmy Carter and Walter Mondale marks the start of a new political era. For the first time in eight years, the Presidency and the Congress are under the control of the same party, providing hope that legislative stalemate and government-by-veto may be finished."[1]

Tom Wicker wrote that "Jimmy Carter may be coming into the White House in January with the best prospects for achieving a legislative program since the Johnson administration took over in 1965. With that one exception, in fact, Mr. Carter's legislative outlook probably is the best for any new president since 1948." Wicker noted that the Democrats held nearly as many seats in the House as they had in 1965, that they also held a 62–38 Senate majority, and that large Democratic majorities in Congress undercut the old House coalition of Republicans and southern Democrats. Finally, reformed congressional procedures made it "easier for legislation to be properly considered and brought to the floor for action."[2]

U.S. News reported that Carter would "find the new Congress readier than any in the last eight years to cooperate with the White House."[3] The news magazine also predicted that large Democratic majorities and the erosion of power of committee chairmen in Congress would facilitate party governance.[4] A few weeks later its optimism overflowed: "For the first time since the mid-1960s, a large degree of harmony between Congress and the White House is in the cards for the new year. The heavy atmosphere of stalemate that has hung over Washington since 1969 is lifting, now that Democrats once again are to be in command at both ends of Pennsylvania Avenue. . . . A new spirit of cooperation seems guaranteed."[5]

To the extent that observers discounted the inevitability of efficient party governance in 1977, they mostly did so because of reservations about Carter's leadership.[6] But by the end of 1977, it had become evident that the expectations for presidential-congressional cooperation were not going to be fulfilled. Conflicts had erupted over presidential appointments, energy policy, tax policy, pork-barrel projects, and even interbranch protocol. Press coverage of Congress's role in the failure of party governance followed the curve of disintegrating harmony.

By the end of 1977, *U.S. News* noted Congress's "degree of independence from the White House that defies the predictions of amity voiced early in the year." The article expressed surprise at congressional demonstrations of unpredictability and independence and attributed these characteristics to the postreform institutional "habit" of challenging presidential power.[7] A few weeks later, *U.S. News* concluded that "Congress's Democratic majorities proved in 1977 that they are not about to be led by the nose by any Chief Executive, Democrat or not, especially when the issues at stake have mobilized powerful special interests with clout in lawmakers' home districts."[8]

What is most striking about the press coverage of legislative-executive conflict in 1977 is the near uniformity of opinion that Carter deserved most of the blame. Journalists thought of Congress as an institution that must be led effectively by the president in order to get anything done. Without presidential leadership, there would be stalemate.[9] The press did not look to Congress for leadership.

Most journalists believed that Congress's contribution to the legislative stalemate stemmed from the congressional reforms of the 1970s. Despite earlier assessments that the reforms created an environment for presidential-congressional cooperation, they seemed to have harmed the chances of realizing a policy agenda. Furthermore, the press contended, the reformers had felt little deference to anyone, including the president. *Wall Street Journal* congressional correspondent Albert R. Hunt wrote in early 1977 that despite the eagerness for legislative-executive harmony, "habits change slowly and many legislators have grown accustomed to their more assertive roles."[10] He later noted "the growing determination of Congress in recent years to insist that it not be taken for granted by an 'imperial' presidency."[11] *New York Times* deputy Washington bureau chief John Herbers observed that "John F. Kennedy could get congressional consent by appealing to a few leaders who controlled the institution. Now congressional power is fragmented, and members have become more independent."[12]

In April, *U.S. News* assessed the troubled relationship. There was a general perception of ineffective presidential leadership, but there was also a more independent spirit on the part of Congress:

The leadership in Congress . . . is new and eager to assert itself. In addition, the growing independence of younger members often is stronger than party loyalties. Carter also took office at a time when members of Congress had tasted success in wresting back powers that they had let slip to the White House in recent years. Most members are fearful of returning to a subservient role—even under a Democratic president.[13]

In May, *U.S. News* Senior Editor Gerald Parshall wrote that although the president's "special brand of leadership" had much to do with interbranch conflict, changes in Congress had contributed to Carter's difficulties with the legislature. The Vietnam War and Watergate had "touched off a desire in Congress to recapture powers that had been gradually surrendered to the executive branch in decades past. It is a trend that is still running strong, despite the return of the White House to Democratic hands. Two thirds of the Democrats in the House have never served under a Democratic president. They are used to going their own way, and the habit is proving hard to break."[14]

In May, Lou Cannon observed that the many new Democrats elected to Congress had "no intention of approving legislation merely because it carries a presidential stamp or the imprimatur of the leadership." Consequently, "the House is now in many respects the 'open institution' that the reformers of a few years ago wanted to make it. Committees operate with a high degree of independence, the younger members are allowed to talk as well as be seen, and amendments even from the minority are frequently considered on the substantive merits." Although Cannon, too, focused on congressional concerns with Carter's governing style, he noted that the independence asserted by the new House members made it very difficult for legislative leaders to overcome policy stalemate.[15]

Throughout the summer, a great many journalists echoed Cannon's analysis. *Washington Post* reporter Edward Walsh wrote that Carter had so much trouble with the Democratic Congress "mostly because Congress changed during the last eight Republican years—it is much more assertive and independent."[16] Columnist Joseph Kraft traced interbranch conflict in part to "the new spirit pervading the Congress. It is a maverick spirit that features independence over cooperation, getting on over going along, kicking the system over supporting it."[17] A *Newsweek* article reported that "some Democrats, invigorated by a sense of independence, seem ready, even eager, to take on Carter."[18]

In September, the chief of the *U.S. News* congressional reporting staff, Thomas J. Foley, also emphasized the mixed blessings of the 1970s congressional reforms:

The unhorsing of autocratic committee chairmen and general dispersion of power . . . have come at a price. They have complicated the tasks of both Congress's leaders and the White House in hammering out broad national policies. Instead of consulting a handful of senior legislators, the norm only a few years ago, leaders now must cope with an often mercurial throng of 535 lawmakers. The result sometimes is delay and deadlock. It makes Congress look to many Americans like a headless and erratic force thrashing about wildly while national problems fester.[19]

At the end of the first session of the 95th Congress, *U.S. News* reanalyzed why the earlier predictions of interbranch cooperation under one-party rule had proven wrong:

Part of the answer lies in the changing makeup of Congress. Its newer members have only weak ties to their party. They were elected as individuals committed to putting local interests above partisan considerations. . . . As for older lawmakers, a great many became convinced during the Vietnam and Watergate years that Congress had yielded too much power to the White House. . . . Even with a Democrat once again heading the executive branch, the habit of putting a congressional imprint on national policies is proving impossible to break.[20]

A *Time* news story likewise noted that the 95th Congress, "elected in the psychological aftermath of the Vietnam War and Watergate," had undergone a series of profound changes that frustrated earlier hopes for interbranch cooperation.[21]

The press criticized Congress in 1977 for more than its failure to work with the president. Meg Greenfield wrote that the Senate in particular did not work effectively because of its outmoded folkways and rules as well as its "peculiar spirit—its haughtiness, sensitivity to slight and rather grand sense of self." She referred to the Senate as the Club and criticized its "preoccupation with the entitlements and independence and importance of the institution (never mind that it doesn't always look so hot to the public)."[22] Joseph Kraft blamed the Senate's ineffectiveness on its failure to adopt reforms as broad-based as those adopted by the House.[23]

Congress also received close coverage of scandals. *Time* reported that the institution had been "rocked by scandals involving sex and bribes, and widely assailed for accepting a pay raise without facing up to a vote on it."[24] Thomas J. Foley wrote that "this Congress is proving as adept as any in memory at giving itself one black eye after another." He added,

First came the pay raise. It was handled in a way that won lawmakers blame both for taking the raise and for initially refusing to vote on it. Then came the disclosure that for years the House and Senate have been drastically understating the costs of overseas junkets, which have long been a sore point with taxpayers. Next was the blowup over the South Korean bribery scandal, which has filled the air with charges of cover-up and foot dragging. . . . [I]t is no wonder that opinion polls continue to show public confidence in Congress hovering near an all-time low. Many Americans clearly believe that their national legislature is worthy of ridicule and disdain.

Foley pointed out that based on news reporting of Congress, this unflattering portrait of the institution appeared to be true. But, Foley concluded, because of reforms in leadership structure and ethics guidelines, the institution did deserve some praise for being less secretive, more democratic, and less wedded to the seniority system.[25]

The congressional pay raise (from $44,600 to $57,500) generated press criticism for how members handled the matter, even though a number of editorials endorsed the decision.[26] Most criticism focused on what Marvin Stone of *U.S. News* called "the shameless conniving and cowardice that Congress displayed in arranging to raise its pay, without having to vote."[27] The *Washington Post* criticized Congress for behaving "shabbily" in the effort to push the pay raise "without the embarrassment of actually voting for it."[28] As the *Wall Street Journal* intoned, "The hypocrisy of the process is becoming a bit tiresome. While Congressmen obviously feel down deep in their hearts that they are entitled to more money . . . they do not feel equally strongly that anyone should know their views on the subject."[29]

Press coverage of Congress in 1977 generally reinforced the public's conviction that the institution does not work effectively without strong presidential leadership. Journalists identified the congressional reforms of the 1970s as among the sources of problems in presidential-legislative relations. According to the prevailing interpretation, the legislature had become an undisciplined institution incapable of advancing a coherent policy agenda. As for the pay raise Congress awarded itself without publicly voting on it, reporters did not, as they had in 1946, defend the need to pay legislators a decent salary that befits their responsibilities, nor did they emphasize the need to offer the kind of salary that would attract quality people to public service.

ENACTMENT OF THE REAGAN ECONOMIC PROGRAM (1981)

To Ronald Reagan's partisans, the 1980 Republican presidential landslide gave the new administration a mandate to enact sweeping changes in government policy, including strong reductions in spending on domestic programs, strong increases in national defense spending, and deep tax cuts. The unexpected election of a Republican Senate, the able leadership of Senate Majority Leader Howard Baker (R–Tenn.), and the president's skills at public persuasion and building legislative coalitions in the House combined to make possible the smooth passage of the administration's economic programs in 1981.

During the administrations of presidents Gerald Ford and Jimmy Carter, many political analysts had written about the imperiled presidency and the ungovernability of the nation. But with the startling legislative victories in 1981, Reagan's presidency appeared to have refuted the prophecies of endless gridlock. Indeed, Reagan's 1981 triumph on Capitol Hill, reported Charles O. Jones, comprised five more victories:[30]

1. Passage of the Economic Recovery Tax Act, a multiyear package that projected a reduction of nearly $750 billion;

2. Enactment of a budget-reconciliation resolution designed to reduce domestic spending by over $35 billion;

3. Approval of a defense plan of nearly $200 billion for 1982, less than the president wanted originally, but more than President Carter had proposed;

4. Significant reductions in the Aid to Families with Dependent Children (AFDC) benefits, food stamps, certain antipoverty programs, and other minor welfare benefits;

5. Savings in Medicaid and Medicare programs, but postponement of an overhauling of the Social Security retirement system.

As usual, Washington reporting of these events focused much more on the presidency than on Congress. Still, a good many press reports and analyses examined Congress's performance in 1981.

For its role in approving the Reagan economic program, Congress received press criticism for failing to be an assertive opponent to the president and failing to act responsibly as the government's budget-making institution. Early in the year, in response to Reagan's aggressive efforts to advance his proposals for budget cuts, the *New York Times* asked, "Where are the Democrats?" The House, led by the opposition party, did not know how to "perform as a coherent opposition." House members were more interested "in protecting one ox or another" than in fighting for causes or even defining their values.[31] A month later, the *Times* was troubled that Reagan's economic program was moving through Congress so unchallenged:

> In its eagerness not to test the new president's popularity, the legislators seem to have abandoned altogether their proper role in the making of economic policy. Congress alone can provide an independent, skilled and detailed evaluation of the president's economic program. Until it does, the public loses. . . . Congressional scrutiny need not mean partisan warfare with the White House. . . . It is one thing for Congress to accept the direction and dimension of his program, quite another to abandon its role in determining the detail of policy.

The paper hoped for "more courage" from Congress in challenging the president's economic leadership.[32]

A June editorial in the *Times* recalled that legislators intended the 1974 budget reforms "to give Congress more say over economic policy and more discipline over its own fragmented spending. But the reform was born a colt with shaky legs. Inflation continued to push the budget above the levels that Congress set for itself, and old spending habits were hard to change." The editorial expressed reservations about the budget-reconciliation bill and asked, "Why has Congress gone along so limply? Because the president is thought to be hugely popular and few politicians want to cross him." The editorial compared the sweeping changes of 1981 to those that led to the Great Society programs. It concluded that perhaps the only way to move programs at such a pace was to have an enormously popular president and "a compliant Congress."[33]

A *Wall Street Journal* editorial also looked back at the 1974 budget reforms and concluded that "despite all of its procedural finery, the process has not worked before this year." The *Journal* identified common abuses—stopgap funding measures, phony budget cuts—and concluded that the process outlined by the 1974 reforms could only work "given the right amount of leadership" from the president. The editorial made clear the view that Congress could not exercise responsible budgetary leadership otherwise.[34] A subsequent *Journal* editorial attributed the lack of sound budgetary policy to "a Congress-bureaucrat-lobbyist complex grown increasingly contemptuous of the broad public interest and popular will." The editorial referred to congressional efforts in the 1974 Budget Act to enforce budgetary discipline as a "fraud" and again said that controlling the process required a reassertion of presidential authority.[35]

David Broder drew a distinction between an "assertive Congress" and "a Congress ready or able to provide leadership of its own." He also believed that despite earlier reforms, Congress remained unprepared and unable to exercise leadership:

> Congress has not, in the eight years since it rebelled against Nixon's dictatorship, systematically addressed the conditions that would allow it to fill that leadership gap, either on its own or in tandem with the president. The crucial questions still remain on Congress's own agenda: policy integration vs. jurisdictional fragmentation; party loyalty vs. individual autonomy; national perspective vs. parochial representation.[36]

Congressional Democrats were often singled out for not being aggressive opponents of Reagan's programs. "The Democrats," Hobart Rowen wrote, "have thrown in the towel. Reagan is an authentic American hero, and the Democrats don't have the stomach for fighting him."[37] Haynes Johnson, reacting to the common label of Reagan as the King of Congress, said, "So he is, for the moment. The Democrats, if not exactly his loyal subjects, are his serfs. They are his to command. The president has his way on all he wishes. He shatters the ranks of his opponents, and leaves them in the position of political supplicants."[38] George F. Will gloated that "the Democrats' ideas are the crumbs of Republican ideas." Rather than propose substantially different economic policies, they merely tried to modify Reagan's programs.[39] Martin Tolchin noted the widespread criticism of House Democrats "for passivity in the face of the most massive single spending reduction in the nation's history."[40] At the end of the year, when it became clear that the nation had to prepare for a sharp economic downturn and unprecedented budget deficits in 1982, the *Washington Post* concluded that "Congress must accept some blame for the present dilemma. It swallowed the administration's economic program nearly whole last summer—and then threw in some extra tax cuts for good measure."[41]

It is clear that in looking for leadership from the federal government, journalists look instinctively to the White House. They look to Congress as a collection of individuals dedicated to parochial interests and self-serving causes. Steven V. Roberts explained, "Capitol Hill is a maze of vested interests and power centers, each with its own motives, and priorities." Legislators favored budget cutting in theory, but "they all howl when their own programs get axed."[42] Congress was generally criticized for ignoring national needs. The *Wall Street Journal* editorialized, "Sure, we know that

Congress people have to think about their next election. But we expect them to think about the general weal, too."[43] At the end of 1981, David Broder explained what members of Congress would face when meeting constituents in their districts:

> Show a little pity for Senator Spender and Congressman Contracts.... This Congress has been a horror show for them.... Not one new program, not one new agency, not one rotten little pilot project they can pin on the wall and send out a press release to brag about.... [David Stockman is] whipping around the Democrats like Spender and Contracts and their staff as if they weren't the best-fed, best-paid, best-equipped Congress in the world.[44]

The most critical review came from a *Wall Street Journal* editorial, "The Treason of Congress," that charged that Congress "has let spending run out of hand, relied on unlegislated tax increases and phony bookkeeping for any semblance of budget balance, driven the nation's largest trust fund to the verge of bankruptcy, and, when confronted with a national mandate to change its ways, thrown up its hands at the 'political difficulty' of reform." The *Journal* referred to Congress as "subservient . . . to the bidding of special interests." The *Journal* summarized the litany of press criticisms that the Congress was privileged, out of touch, and incompetent:

> Congress lives in an isolated, self-indulgent universe, oblivious to the way its rhetoric translates into the real world. . . . Pampered, privileged, surrounded by aides who regard him with servile contempt, your Congressman has become adept at confusing the public good with his own interest and interests. Campaign reforms become a means for protecting incumbents. Budget outlays become a mutual aid arrangement with budget constituencies. The duty to the folks back home becomes a matter of winning them federal goodies, to the point that it is a question whether the Congressman is serving his electors or corrupting them. . . . Congress has sold us out.[45]

In 1981, then, to the extent that the federal government was applauded for advancing an aggressive domestic agenda, credit accrued to the Reagan administration. To the extent that members of the press reported Congress's performance on domestic matters, they blamed it for failing to challenge the president or for obstructing his leadership. Press reviews reinforced the common perception that the nation's legislature was incapable of leadership, primarily in business for itself, and not attuned to national interests and needs.

TAX REFORM (1986)

Perhaps the most far-reaching achievement of the 99th Congress was its passage of a major tax-reform law. Some considered the law the most sweeping tax reform legislation ever. As adopted, the law removed several million working poor from the tax rolls; eliminated numerous tax "loopholes"; and created a somewhat simplified tax rate structure.

During the early stage of congressional action, many expressed skepticism that Congress would move beyond special-interest politics to enact a tax-reform package. Rowland Evans and Robert Novak described members of the Senate as "eager accomplices of the capital's best-paid lobbyists."[46] Much of the criticism focused on the actions of the Senate Finance Committee and its chairman, Bob Packwood (R–Oreg.). During markup of the bill, Packwood and other members sought to preserve tax-reduction benefits for certain industries. "Vested interests die hard," said the *New York Times*. The committee was undermining "invigorating change."[47] The committee instead was creating "a Christmas tree" full of special privileges.[48] Committee members had "demonstrated in public their fealty to the interest groups hovering around the bill."[49]

When the committee passed its version of tax reform, with fewer privileges than earlier anticipated, the *Times* gleamed, "Wonderful." To move the initiative to enactment, "Congress will have to do something it's not good at: Recognize the virtue of sacrificing individual interests for the common good."[50] The *Post* expressed amazement that the committee had "done a pretty amazing thing" in approving tax reform. "Maybe Halley's Comet did it."[51]

As members of both houses worked out a bipartisan plan, *Newsweek* reported that the legislators had "praised themselves for not doing business as usual."[52] The *Times* implored Senate conferees under pressure from lobbyists "to grit their teeth and put [the] national interest first."[53] That a compromise emerged after intense lobby pressure, reported E. J. Dionne, Jr., "made the end result seem all the more extraordinary."[54] That Congress overcame its usual obstacles, reported David E. Rosenbaum, must have resulted from "peculiar political circumstances."[55]

By early summer, it had become evident that Congress would enact tax reform. One member told *Newsweek* that "we'll do the work. But you can be sure that Ronald Reagan will get the credit."[56] Tom Wicker asked, "Who gets the credit?" Although the initiative was "the product of both parties and of Congress and the President," he answered that Reagan would get most of the credit: "His Administration's proposals started the drive for revision, he campaigned hard for it when few others would, and at the inevitable signing ceremony in the White House, it'll be he—not Dan Rostenkowski or Tip O'Neill—at center screen."[57]

These predictions proved mostly correct. Just prior to enactment, the *Times* gave first credit to Reagan and then some to congressional leaders who pushed for reform.[58] On the day that Reagan signed what the paper called "the biggest and best tax reform in decades," its editorial gave "a full measure of credit" to the president and additional credit to congressional leaders.[59] David Broder wrote that Congress had succeeded because of Reagan's leadership and cooperation. Congress had failed to achieve much in those areas in which its members resisted presidential leadership.[60] Gerald M. Boyd reported that the initiative would be remembered as a Reagan legislative triumph. It was the president's efforts to drive the legislative process that moved the Congress.[61] Steven V. Roberts largely credited the president's initiative and savvy at defining the issue for public debate. His leadership helped to overcome the usual patterns on Capitol Hill that stifle reform.[62]

Although press coverage praised tax reform, many questioned whether Congress would not revert to type and undo the progress. The *Times* expressed concern that lobby pressure would lead Congress in the 100th session "to undo major accomplishments that don't sit well with influential taxpayers."[63] According to the paper, "Members of Congress can't see past narrow interests."[64] The *Wall Street Journal* was even less restrained when it editorialized that after Congress had for years given special tax breaks, it "will try to do it again, provided of course its members feel they can get away with it." The *Journal* advised, "Enjoy it while you can. Congress will be back on Jan. 6 and the movement to take away tax reform will start. . . . The raw material for the rollback is all too evident in Congress's thought process, with its always-insatiable appetite for more revenues, its professed panic over the deficit, and in the staggered, static-analysis view of tax reform."[65]

At the end of the 99th Congress, *U.S. News* surveyed editorial opinion of the legislature's performance: "better than average" for its efforts on tax reform, immigration, Superfund, and antidrug policy, but in handling the budget deficit, "a great big red F." Although some praised the tax-reform initiative as truly significant, editorial opinion reflected an unenthusiastic view of Congress's leadership.[66]

In reviewing the tax-reform initiative, journalists reinforced the view that Congress worked best under the guiding hand of strong presidential leadership. They also characterized the legislators as too beholden to special interests. That Congress succeeded at enacting a tax-reform program resulted in high praises for the president's initiative and expressions of delight, yet surprise, that Congress had overcome special-interest pressures. Congress received perhaps less credit than it deserved for its efforts, and by the end of the 99th Congress, most editorialists gave the session either mixed or poor reviews.

THE IRAN-CONTRA INVESTIGATIONS (1986–1987)

In November 1986, the nation learned that with President Reagan's approval, the United States had sold weapons to Iran. Some of the proceeds had been diverted to the Nicaraguan contra movement in violation of the Boland amendment, which prohibited the use of federal funds to aid the contras. The president insisted that he neither approved nor even knew about the diversion carried out by his administration.

Congress established House and Senate select committees to investigate the controversy. Televised hearings lasted forty-one days in the summer of 1987. Congress called thirty-two witnesses, the most important of whom were National Security Council Adviser John Poindexter and Lieutenant Colonel Oliver North. The hearings were the most publicly visible displays of Congress's investigatory powers since its Watergate performance.

The image of the congressional investigation created by the press was not the image of the courageous legislature restoring the constitutional balance of power during Watergate. Throughout the controversy, liberal voices in the press complained that the legislators were not challenging the executive vigorously enough. Conservative journalists charged them with eroding the president's authority to conduct foreign policy.

Early in the controversy, Congress received some encouragement to get involved in the investigations. The *Washington Post* called for a "broad inquiry" because the office of the independent counsel could not do the job alone. The *Post* recommended that special congressional committees hold public hearings "into questions of public policy, foreign relations and ethics that are at the heart of the matter and beyond the jurisdiction of an independent counsel."[67] Tom Wicker added that Congress had "to inquire into the real extent of Mr. Reagan's dereliction. . . . All that's needed is a tough and relentless investigation."[68] A few weeks earlier, however, Wicker had been uncertain whether Congress was tough enough to challenge presidential authority. If precedent was a guide, Congress would avoid the serious issues and defer to presidential national security powers.[69]

New York Times reporter Linda Greenhouse considered the inquiries as an opportunity and a challenge for Congress to unravel the controversy and strengthen its foreign policy power.[70] Steven V. Roberts identified another challenge—and potential pitfall. "By investigating and evaluating a major element of the Administration's foreign policy, the committees represent an important assertion of congressional influence over the executive branch and threaten to tip the balance of power in Washington toward Capitol Hill."[71]

A number of conservative journalists expressed strong reservations about Congress's role in the investigations. Norman Podhoretz believed that the balance of power had already been tipped in Congress's favor. Congress had been "handed, and happily seized, an opportunity to mount an assault on the presidency. . . . An Imperial Congress [was] attempting to make [foreign] policy instead of consenting to or opposing presidential initiatives." He warned that "a body as large and diverse as Congress can never run an activist foreign policy: mostly it can obstruct and delay."[72] James Kilpatrick speculated that the congressional investigations would "manifest the inefficiency that infects [Congress] as a whole. Why two separate committees? Why not one joint committee. The answer, gentle reader, is that two committees require twice the staff and generate twice the publicity than would be true of one committee." Summing up his opinions of Congress, Kilpatrick growled, "The inefficiency is appalling; the rules are archaic; the waste of time is incredible. If American industry ran its affairs as sloppily as the U.S. Congress ran its affairs, American industry would go broke in six weeks. As the 100th Congress convenes, it may be timely to voice an urgent plea to members: cut out the fun and games and get down to work."[73]

Wall Street Journal columnist Suzanne Garment believed that the impetus to investigate Iran-contra derived from a mindless pattern of responding to every crisis as though it were the next Watergate. She feared that Congress might enact more rules restricting presidential policymaking in foreign affairs.[74] George F. Will cited the familiar criticism that Congress was unable to keep secrets. He believed that it needed to grant immunity to North and Poindexter to ensure that the full story would be told, unless, of course, "it is television rather than truth that Congress craves."[75]

The *Wall Street Journal* persistently criticized Congress for meddling where it did not belong. An editorial in February 1987 stated, "The core of this country's difficulties in foreign policy is that many members of the Washington community have adopted the quite radical position that Congress not only has powers to debate and fund foreign policy but is entitled to engage itself directly in policy execution. That is a prescription for paralysis. The Founding Fathers . . . vested primary responsibility for foreign affairs in the president."[76] A week later, the paper iterated the view: "Put bluntly, much of the blame for this fiasco goes to dangerous and perhaps unconstitutional attempts by Congress to regulate how the executive branch conducts foreign policy. Time and again, the 248–page [Tower Commission Report] traces the root source of the mistakes in the Iran-contra affair to congressional interference with normal executive branch activities. The president made mistakes, but partly because his advisers felt constrained by congressional legislation from advising him."[77]

On May 5, 1987, the first day of the televised congressional hearings, the *Journal* declared the Boland amendment "patently unconstitutional" and added that "much of the problem of Iranian policy results from the contortions of trying to run a policy in the face of congressional restrictions of dubious constitutionality."[78] One week later, it stated that "these months of hearings will be worth the effort if congressmen are forced to take their fair share of the blame." Therefore, members of the Iran-contra committees framed the issues on legalistic rather than policy terms so that they would not "have to accept some of the blame for policies gone awry."[79]

Washington Post reporters Dan Morgan and Walter Pincus stated that "Congress also is on trial." In their view, "Congress is in a special position because its past failure to exercise vigorous oversight means it shares some responsibility for what happened."[80]

As Congress proceeded with the hearings, press criticism persisted. Charles Krauthammer asserted that "the air of moral superiority of some congressional inquisitors is hard to take. Contra policy has not exactly been Congress's finest hour. In fact, there is not one congressional contra policy but five." He further criticized Congress's performance in the controversy:

If Congress were a person, it should be recalled for such conduct—subject perhaps to its version of the 25th amendment, which allows for relief from duty owing to demonstrated mental incapacity. But Congress isn't a person. It is a shifting coalition of interests and factions. Precisely for this reason it ought to be circumspect about conducting foreign policy, particularly regarding an issue on which it has shown itself to be incapable of defining a minimally coherent policy. There is a reason why the Constitution assigns primary responsibility for the conduct of foreign policy to the president and not to Congress. The Boland saga is a case study.[81]

Linda Greenhouse reported that because of North's skillful testimony, the televised hearing had become "the scourge of Congress." Rather than appearing statesmanlike, members of the investigating committees "appeared off stride, scrambling to regain momentum and public credibility."[82]

Although much of the press criticism of Congress's handling of the investigations came from conservative political observers,[83] more liberal journalists also found its performance unimpressive. *Washington Post* columnist Mary McGrory lambasted Congress for not acting more decisively to prevent the controversy:

You listen to Congress's record on the contra war—no, yes, maybe—and you wonder, what were [the Founding Fathers] thinking of to confer the power of the purse on foreign policy on such a collection? . . . Congress eventually, in spite of itself, got wind of it all. What did the great, slow-moving, cowardly beast do? Well, nothing, actually. . . . The membership of the select committee is sown with closet monarchists who long for trumpets and ermine and royal edicts. They think the founders were dead wrong to give people like themselves the right to rein in a giant such as Ronald Reagan.[84]

In another column, McGrory declared that Congress had nearly become irrelevant to the conduct of foreign policy. She described Congress as a feeble, almost irrelevant institution when compared to the presidency:

Why do we have a Congress? We have one because the Constitution says we must. What does Congress do? Well, the members serve as extras in presidential specials. Try to imagine the State of the Union without all those bodies. . . . Also, they perform small services for constituents. They send them baby books, copies of speeches, appeals for money . . . [and] dispense tickets to the galleries, where citizens can watch legislators not legislate.

When it came to serious policy matters, she commented, Congress was more interested in grandstanding than in genuine accomplishment. "It holds hearings, summons witnesses, pontificates, marks up, postures through long debates, haggles with the White House, temporizes, compromises and, if it passes the tattered shreds of what it had in mind, pats itself on the back."[85]

The *Post*'s David Ignatius believed that Congress appeared weak and unable to assert its authority in the wake of North's testimony. Committee members "rush[ed] to the network interview booths to say what a persuasive witness North had been" after he admitted that he had lied to Congress and shredded government documents. Ignatius speculated that the Iran-contra committees would issue a "blistering final report criticizing the president" and that Congress would pass a new statute to try to control covert activities. "But none of these steps will go to the heart of the matter—which is to deter abuse of presidential power." Ignatius attributed the "acquiescence of a bootless Congress" to the view that some intelligence operations are beyond the realm of law.[86]

Meg Greenfield acknowledged that if North charmed the public by playing to the television cameras, "so in large measure was the committee playacting. I think viewers knew this, sensed at once that there is something *not quite jake* about the committee procedure as advertised, and so they were disposed to favor the witness who seemed to beat the interrogators at their own game."[87] James Reston wrote that the Iran-contra controversy was telling evidence of the lack of "that sense of trust between the White House and Congress that is the essential ingredient of democratic government." He believed that the congressional hearings had failed to restore the ingredient of trust between the political branches.[88] *Newsweek* described the various problems created when Congress tried to assert its authority to make foreign policy.

Congress can rarely initiate foreign policy; much more often it re-acts—and all too often overreacts, as it may have done in 1976 when it imposed a blanket ban on U.S. aid to rebels in Angola. In other cases Congress hedges with vaguely worded legislation—like the Boland amendment restricting U.S. aid to the contras—registering its disap-proval but avoiding a clear "no." In still other instances oversight becomes "micromanagement": the House has voted to dictate what kind of wine to serve at embassy receptions and interfered with decisions about closing consulates. . . . The Iran-contra revelations point sharply to the need for congressional review. Legislators can also help the president build public support for policies that may be dimly understood. The problem is that congressional review often shades into congressional direction.[89]

Few journalists praised Congress's efforts in the Iran-contra hearings. Haynes Johnson did report that "not since the Vietnam war has there been so serious a debate about the respective constitutional roles and responsibilities of the legislative and executive branches of government." The hearings, he said, had at least provided "a wealth of new information."[90] In another column, Johnson applauded the committee members who, on the fifth day of North's testimony, made appeals for a stronger public understanding of the constitutional issues at stake in the controversy:

> The result was an outpouring of expressions of democratic values. This was no "cave-of-the-winds" kind of political rhetoric common in the hot air of Congress. . . . This was serious exposition of greater public purposes and of the proper workings of the constitutional system, expressed memorably and movingly. . . . Whatever else lies ahead, the Iran-contra hearings have accomplished their central purpose. They have provided what cynics said could not happen: a public forum, held in the most visible arena, in which a genuine debate about basic democratic principles and values has taken place.[91]

At the end of the hearings in August, however, Johnson offered a less affirmative interpretation: "Despite fascinating hearings that produced extraordinary information . . . in the end, the hearings were as untidy and as inconclusive—if also as essential—as the democratic process itself. Some of the questioning was sloppy, and many leads were never pursued. By allowing North to dictate the terms of his appearance, the panels opened themselves to second-guessing that will undoubtedly continue for years."[92]

Of all the press reviews of Congress's performance, none was more favorable than that of a *New York Times* editorial:

> Congress has just completed three months of hearings that have served the nation brilliantly. The investigating committees . . . affirm American democracy. The process proves the political system's strength, not its fragility. It counters abuse of power, and holds those who abused trust accountable. It deters future leaders who might be tempted to transform their election or appointment into limitless mandates for unlawful action. . . . Congress, proceeding with abundant fairness, had many of its finest hours upholding the Constitution's integrity.[93]

But the *Wall Street Journal* continued to offer blistering criticism. It characterized the majority report of the Iran-contra committees as "masterful political advocacy." The editorial continued,

> The congressmen faced the daunting task of somehow beating up on President Reagan after clearing him of lying or lawbreaking. The congressmen didn't flinch. They stared hypocrisy straight in the face and didn't blink once in their report's 427 pages. . . . The most bald-faced hypocrisy is the idea that Congress wants President Reagan to be more aggressive in enforcing the laws. Clearly, the more damaging act against public trust is congressional mangling of its own budget rules. Congress, after all, voted publicly for Gramm-Rudman. When it couldn't abide by its deficit targets, it changed them. . . . Maybe President Reagan should call executive hearings on congressional noncompliance.[94]

The *Journal* regarded the major outcome of the congressional investigations as "an undesirable, and potentially dangerous . . . weakened presidency." By acting to humiliate the president, the Congress allegedly had vaulted its own interests above those of the country. The editorial characterized Congress as an institution that fostered inflationary policies and protectionist laws, conducted a "smear campaign" against a distinguished Supreme Court nominee, and undermined the cause of a democratic movement in Central America.[95] The *Journal* referred to the committees' members as "the commander in chief pretenders of Congress" and scorned the "overbearing congressional meddling in [presidential] foreign affairs powers." Finally, it summed up, "the unconstitutional usurpation by Congress of the executive's foreign-policy powers is necessary to explain the Iran-contra 'scandal.' "[96]

Before the hearings had begun, *U.S. News* had described Congress as "increasingly intrusive in foreign affairs."[97] After their conclusion, it expressed disappointment that, in effect, Congress had not been intrusive enough: "What emerged from the weeks of televised hearings was not a complete or fully coherent narrative but, rather, a jumbled puzzle with many of its pieces missing. In many instances, witnesses' assertions went unchallenged, contradictions were not cleared up and key questions were not answered; as to the money from the arms sales, which so intrigued investigators at the outset, some still couldn't be found."[98]

U.S. News editor-in-chief Mortimer B. Zuckerman had earlier summed up what needed to be done: Congress had "to examine its own role in two respects." First, the institution needed a small joint oversight committee to remove any excuse for executive-branch secrecy. Second,

> Congress has to recognize that its role in foreign policy requires consistency and candor. Members have a deplorable tendency to pass legislation that gives them protection on both sides of difficult issues. For example, the requirement that the president notify Congress of covert actions "in a timely fashion" is a deliberate ambiguity. Congress should make the time limit precise. The Boland Amendment forbidding federal aid to the contras was also ambiguous in its terms.[99]

Thus, despite having taken the initiative in investigating the Iran-contra affair, Congress received generally unfavorable press commentary for exposing executive-branch wrongdoing and for trying to restore balance to interbranch relations in foreign policymaking. At times during the hearings, the press portrayed Congress as feeble in its efforts to hold the perpetrators of the controversy accountable; at other times, as intrusive and grandstanding. Commentaries focused on familiar criticisms of Congress: lack of leadership, failure to act vigorously and efficiently, inability to conduct a coherent and consistent foreign policy, holding public hearings merely to get publicity, and using hearings for partisan purposes to embarrass the president and weaken his presidency.

FEDERAL PAY-RAISE PROPOSAL (1988–1989)

The presidential Commission on Executive, Legislative, and Judicial Salaries examined the issue of federal pay in 1988. Led by attorney Lloyd Cutler, the commission concluded that salaries for federal appointees, judges, and members of Congress had become inadequate. The commission maintained that real pay for the top-level federal workers had eroded 35 percent since 1969. Because of this, top-quality people were no longer easily attracted to public service, and many—especially federal judges— were leaving the public sector at an alarming rate. The commission noted that the cost of living in the Washington, D.C., area, combined with much higher salary potential in the private sector, made it necessary to offer a very substantial pay increase to the top-level federal officers.

The commission consequently recommended a 51 percent pay increase for approximately 3,000 of these officials, including members of Congress. President Reagan included the commission's recommendation in the fiscal-year 1990 budget, meaning that the pay increase would automatically be implemented on February 8, 1989, unless voted down by both houses of Congress.

The proposal resulted in a firestorm of protest directed against the Congress. The most vocal opponents of the pay raise were consumer activist Ralph Nader and a number of talk-radio hosts who egged on an angry public. Elite press commentary contributed to the tide of anger. Three themes dominated the commentary: (1) the pay raise was either too high or not deserved at all; (2) the process of allowing a pay raise without a congressional vote was indefensible; (3) members of Congress were less deserving of a pay increase than other federal workers.

The news weeklies drubbed Congress for initially moving to let the pay increase take effect. A *Time* report dismissed the commission's argument that members of Congress, with annual salaries of $89,500, suffered financial difficulties from maintaining two residences. Seats in Congress "never go begging" for candidates, "and few incumbents ever retire because of financial straits." *Time* called the fringe benefits of members "cushy enough to provoke the envy of all but the best compensated private executives."[100] According to the magazine's reporting, a House proposal to eliminate speaking honoraria for members once the pay increase went into effect was "an attempt to mollify the 98 percent of the populace that earns less than members of Congress." A proposal by House Speaker, Jim Wright (D–Tex.), to scale back the proposed pay increase to 30 percent and to eliminate the honoraria was a "disingenuous scheme."[101] Walter Shapiro of *Time* more directly described Congress's performance in the "Great Salary Grab" as "cowardice," "duplicitous," "running for cover," and "chicken." He wrote: "In an ideal world, these legislators-for-life would reward the faithful electorate with an impressive display of bravery and statesmanlike behavior. So much for naive theory."[102]

Newsweek called the pay-raise proposal a "miraculous bonanza," Speaker Wright the "wagon boss of the gravy train," and Congress's behavior the result of "rich lodes of greed, cowardice and hypocrisy." Why should members of Congress get a big pay raise when "they enjoy a wide range of perks from lavish pensions to cheap haircuts"? "As [Senator] Gordon Humphrey put it, adult America is already fed up; the problem is what the children will think. 'We run from accountability,' he said, 'as cockroaches run from the bright light.' Nobody has put it better."[103] *Newsweek* reports characterized Congress's efforts as attempts to "avoid accountability." To the average wage earner, "a six-figure salary seems rosy, indeed."[104] *U.S. News* compared Thomas Jefferson's proposal two centuries earlier to pay legislators two bushels of wheat per day to the 1988 commission's proposal of $135,000 per year (or 187 bushels per day).105

Columnists weighed in with their criticisms of Congress. Some said that members did not deserve any raise. Colman McCarthy marveled at how these public servants, among the top 2 percent of wage earners, could justify needing a 51 percent pay increase. Public service should not, he argued, be rewarded with high wages. Furthermore, "High wages paid to public officials hasn't [*sic*] bought integrity." He deplored the various rewards to members: "benefits, pensions, junkets, honoraria, freebies," and "leftover campaign gold at the end of the congressional rainbow."106

Judy Mann wrote that "managers who run up that kind of [budget] deficit in the private sector don't get pay raises. They get canned." She believed that working people were duly outraged both by the size of the proposed raise and the method of enacting it.107 Jack Anderson and Dale Van Atta added that such a proposal "at a time when the budget is seriously out of balance is an affront to all Americans." Average wage earners had a right to be angry. "Many members of Congress come to Washington at great personal sacrifice, and all they ask is a chance to serve their country—for a six-figure income."108

Charles Krauthammer called Congress's efforts a "grotesque example" of avoiding responsibility. "Congress has developed a remarkable capacity for cowardice."109 Richard Cohen agreed that by avoiding a vote, Congress had shown no leadership or courage. Cohen perceived good reasons for the pay raise but concluded that it was unseemly for members to try to achieve that objective through the device of a commission instead of a public defense of the principle and an open vote on the proposal.110

The conspicuous exception to much of the negative commentary was David Broder's argument in favor of the full pay raise. He decried the "cockeyed populism" of anti–pay-raise arguments and worried that uncompetitive salaries diminished "the quality and integrity of government."111

Editorialists had their own critical spin on the proposal. The *Wall Street Journal* approved of federal pay raises for the executive and judicial branches only: "Perhaps the most shocking feature of federal pay is that Congress decided to attach its own dead weight to the pay of the two branches of government that still function. There's no reason in the world that federal judges and executive-branch officials should have to pay for the PR problems Congress created for itself with its scandals and PAC messes."112 The *Journal* bluntly stated that "there is a good case to be made for stiffing Congress and helping the others." That case was not allowing the other branches "to sink to the level of competence the public so

vociferously discerns in the legislative branch." The newspaper also lambasted the use of a commission as a typical "Machiavellian" congressional
tactic to avoid accountability. "How about a Citizen's Commission on
Congressional Reform? Members could be picked at random by throwing
a dart at state tax rolls."[113]

The *Washington Post* considered the proposed pay raise "too generous"
and criticized the "dissembling, the indirect, no-fingerprints and nearly
furtive way the thing is to be done." The paper liked the proposal to
eliminate honoraria but believed that this issue should have been treated
separately.[114] "It's the wrong way to proceed. W-R-O-N-G."[115] Although
critical of the process, the paper believed that some level of pay increase
was justified. "It shames them as individuals and as an institution" not to
openly vote on the raise.[116]

The *New York Times* agreed. "The members must either find the courage
to raise their salaries openly or live on what they now get." The paper also
believed that Congress should ban honoraria and not link the issue to a pay
raise.[117] Like the *Post*, the *Times* supported some form of pay increase, but
believed that Congress had pursued the idea the wrong way.[118]

Public opinion overwhelmingly opposed the pay raise. A poll by the
Gallup Organization showed 82 percent opposition to a pay increase, even
though the question alerted respondents that Congress had coupled that
proposal with one to eliminate honoraria. Gallup analysts suggested that
low public regard for Congress generally had much to do with that result.[119]

Congress retreated from the plan to allow the pay increase to go into
effect without a vote. After the enormous upheaval, the House and Senate
voted overwhelmingly against the pay increase.[120] David Broder blasted
Congress for giving up the raise in the face of "know-nothing demagogu-
ery." He criticized the press's "shabby" coverage of the issue. "Editorial
writers who should have known better, including those on *The Post*, chose
to take cheap shots."[121]

Congress would take up the pay raise again in 1989. To put it mildly,
members were stunned by the venomous response to the initial proposal.
Coverage of the pay-raise failure in 1988 and early 1989 foreshadowed
some of the most debilitating, cynical press treatment of the institution in
the early 1990s. Ultimately the House of Representatives approved a pay
increase combined with new limits on honoraria in November 1989. The
plan raised members' salaries to $96,600 in 1990 and $125,100 in 1991 once
all honoraria were banned. Because of another public and media outcry, the
Senate failed to approve a similar plan, and its members' salaries lagged

behind those of House members for a few years. In July 1991, once again to howls of protest, the Senate put its pay scale on a parity with the House.

THE MIDDLE EAST CRISIS (1990–1991)

After Iraq's invasion of Kuwait on August 2, 1990, President George Bush put together an international coalition to back U.N. Resolution 678 authorizing economic sanctions against Iraq and backed resolutions supporting the use of force in the Persian Gulf if Iraq failed to leave Kuwait. Although the president showed considerable diplomatic skill in building the international coalition, he experienced difficulty in developing a bipartisan congressional coalition to support potential U.S. actions against Iraq. For weeks before his ultimatum to Iraq to remove its forces from Kuwait by January 15, 1991, Congress appeared mired in uncertainty over whether to debate U.S. policy in the Persian Gulf, to oppose military action and support only diplomatic efforts and economic sanctions, to fully support the president's actions, or to issue a formal declaration of war.

The president was reluctant to seek congressional approval for the authority to take military action against Iraq. He was concerned that a vote against granting the authority could undermine both constitutionally and politically his authority to act. Congress, despite having agonized over the appropriate course of action, debated the issue of further sanctions versus granting war powers until just before the January 15 deadline. On January 12, it granted the president—by votes of 52 to 47 in the Senate and 250 to 183 in the House—the authority to wage war against Iraq to expel its military from Kuwait.[122]

Press coverage of Congress during these months was concentrated in the weeks leading up to the House and Senate debates and the days immediately after the congressional vote on January 12, 1991. Before the debates, the press criticized Congress for not asserting its authority to help make foreign policy. There was a strong consensus that Congress had a legitimate and necessary role in the decision of whether to go to war. "Congress should share the responsibility of a decision as grave as this one," Anthony Lewis wrote,[123] and he later implored Congress not to abdicate its constitutional authority to declare war.[124]

George F. Will agreed: "Now that there soon may be 400,000 U.S. personnel in the Persian Gulf region, it is time to involve 535 other Americans." Will believed that Congress could help to "clarify U.S. policy" and that "only Congress can legitimize offensive action with forces this numerous." The conservative columnist warned about the danger of "a war begun with unclear goals and uncertain domestic support. Congress should be convened to listen, watch, learn, clarify and legitimize."[125] Later he argued that the potential political damage to the president of a weak majority vote in Congress was unimportant. The larger issue was one of "due deliberation" and "constitutional propriety." Congress, therefore, must debate and decide.[126] Nor was the involvement in decisionmaking constitutionally ambiguous. The day before the vote was taken, Will asserted:

> Constitutionally, Congress must authorize any launching, from a standing start, of one of the largest military operations in American history. Authorization does not mean after-the-fact ratification. Authorization must be formal and explicit, not merely inferred from legislative silence or statements by individual legislators or collateral legislative activity. Congress must do this even though many members are eager to flee from responsibility. It is a duty, not a perquisite.[127]

Charles Krauthammer had earlier written much the same, but with less rhetorical balance. Congress, he said, was shirking its responsibility by not deciding either to support or oppose the president's actions. "The president should call Congress back into session immediately, present it with a resolution authorizing the use of force and make the gutless wonders choose."[128] He noted elsewhere that the president's actions in the Middle East, including the massive military buildup in Saudi Arabia, were tantamount to "an executive declaration of war. In America, however, the legislature is supposed to declare war." Krauthammer elaborated:

> Congress has a legitimate and essential role to play in the affair. The issue is not just constitutional. It is political. War cannot be waged successfully without popular support. If Congress is not consulted, it will simply criticize, fatally compromising any military action that runs into the slightest difficulty or delay. . . . It is important for Congress to declare itself on the Gulf as soon as possible. The operative word is "declare." Expressing itself, gassing off about the agony of it all, simply won't do. The country needs decisions. The worst thing Congress can do is simply to debate the issue without resolving it—i.e., without coming to a vote on the use of force.[129]

Congressional resolution drew out a spectrum of press commentary that reflected the themes sounded by Will and Krauthammer. "For Congress the issue now seems to have become one of whether the wimp mantle has been passed from George Bush to Capitol Hill," Nathaniel C. Nash wrote,[130] and he was echoed by Mary McGrory in a column entitled "The Hill's Own Wimp Factor," which outlined options available to Congress to play a more substantive role in Persian Gulf policymaking. She referred to the members of Congress as "too insecure" to use their rightful constitutional powers in such a crisis and added that "Congress is a body much given to wringing hands when it is not shaking them, and it has no idea what to do."[131] McGrory criticized Bush for failing to make a clear, consistent, convincing case for the war. Nonetheless, she wrote that "it is not necessary to be eloquent, or even consistent, about war aims as long as the opposition is represented by a Congress that deep down agrees with Bush and Baker that foreign policy is really none of its business."[132]

The editorial pages of the *Washington Post* and the *New York Times* led the charge for more congressional involvement. The *Post* asserted that "Congress must weigh in. It is its political duty and its constitutional obligation." The editorial complained that the Congress had "shrunk from assuming a co-responsibility in this crisis."[133] The *Post* reasoned that the nation could not arrive at a "consensus" on how to handle the foreign policy crisis without congressional debate on the issue. Furthermore, "Congressional involvement alone could produce the kind of intensely sifted judgment suitable to a momentous national undertaking. A president and Congress respectful of the Constitution would not dodge such a debate."[134]

The *Times* expressed concern that the country would go to war "by George Bush's unilateral decision" and countered that "the best place to explain the need to open fire is in Congress, and the best way is to debate a declaration of war."[135] It acknowledged that the president has substantial warmaking authority, "but it is astonishing to claim that all Congress can do is go along. Congress has more authority than that, if only it will reclaim it."[136] As January began, the newspaper became more shrill. Congress had "shirked its constitutional duty to debate a declaration of war." Further delay on a vote would be "unconscionable. While hundreds of thousands of young Americans gird for battle in the deserts of Arabia, their elected representatives can't summon up the courage to confront their responsibilities at home. . . . Debate over the wisdom of war is raging everywhere in America except where it's supposed to—in Congress."[137] Finally, the *Times* turned to mockery. Congressional leaders, it explained, had adopted the "Calhoun strategy."

That refers not to John C. Calhoun of states' rights fame, but to the hard-running fullback on an otherwise hapless football team whose exploits Lyndon Johnson used to recount when he was Senate majority leader.

In one lopsided contest, Calhoun's team was unable to gain any ground. Yet, unaccountably, Calhoun didn't carry the ball once. The coach began yelling, "Give the ball to Calhoun!" To no avail. Time and again his orders went unheeded; time and again his team was thrown for a loss. Exasperated, he called time out. "Why don't you give the ball to Calhoun?" he demanded of his quarterback.

"Cause Calhoun says he don't want it, Coach."[138]

The *Wall Street Journal* registered reactions that mirrored those in the *Washington Post* and *New York Times*.[139] Paul A. Gigot, for example, wrote that "Congress wants to be 'consulted,' as long as it never has to accept any responsibility," and he implored it to stop "niggling" and declare itself by presenting "an up or down vote."[140] George J. Church wrote that "if the U.S. is to fight Iraq, it should be by conscious decision of its elected representatives, reached after full debate."[141] Other commentators also urged Congress to declare either support for or opposition to Bush's war policy.[142]

Once Congress debated and voted, press coverage changed. The institution now received high praise for squarely confronting the crisis and taking a position. Robin Toner explained:

These have not been glory years for Congress. Ethical storms, budget squabbling and the chronic appearance of political deadlock have all left their mark on the image of this proud institution. But over the last few days, as the House and Senate debated whether to authorize the president to go to war in the Persian Gulf, the lawmakers have struggled to step up to what the framers of the Constitution had in mind. One by one, congressmen and senators took the floor and reached for the legacy of history, for Kennedy and Roosevelt and Churchill. They spoke, too, of their children, and the children of their constituents, and of past wars and the lessons they taught. Throughout the debate was the wrenching, sobering consciousness of their own responsibility.[143]

The *New York Times* stated that the "debate over going to war showed how conscientiously Congress can address momentous questions."[144] And Anthony Lewis wrote, "The congressional debate on war in the Persian Gulf paid belated respect to the constitutional system for deciding when America goes to war. It was an impressive debate."[145] E. J. Dionne, Jr., too offered a favorable review of Congress's performance:

After many years in which American politics has been derided for game-playing, sound-bite mongering, narrow partisanship and just plain foolishness, the Persian Gulf debate in the Capitol has proven something surprising: The country's politicians are still capable of carrying out a serious debate on a serious subject with touches of eloquence and all the gravity that the topic of war demands.

After many hours of talking, it was clear that just about everyone had tried to come to grips with the others' arguments, that each side was willing to engage the other with civility and a minimum of name-calling. . . . The course America is about to take may represent genius or folly, but no one will be able to say Congress failed to air the alternatives and debate them with sobriety and conviction.[146]

The most congratulatory review came from David Broder:

One thing on which everyone could agree . . . was that Congress—that familiar whipping boy—had dealt with the issue of authorizing the use of force in a manner befitting the gravity of the subject. The weekend debate was civil and somber, always serious and often eloquent. Senators and representatives dealt respectfully with each other's arguments and showed compassion for the anguish even their opponents felt. The debate served superbly well the requirements of representative government, informing the public and reflecting the electorate's divided views.

Broder identified the conditions that enabled Congress to succeed and implied that these should always be present. First, Congress moved quickly and, despite separation of powers and divided government, placed the president's priority at the top of its agenda. Second, Congress framed the debate clearly so that there would be no doubt about the institution's position. Third, debate time was limited and occurred simultaneously in both legislative chambers. Fourth, legislators, not staffers, wrote the speeches, which were unusually eloquent and heartfelt. Finally, interest groups stayed out of the way, allowing "genuine two-way communication between lawmakers and constituents to take place."[147]

Thus press commentary on Congress before and after the debates was dramatically different. When Congress appeared to recoil from debate over Persian Gulf policy, the press criticized it for failing to assert constitutional powers in a crisis. After the debate, the press praised the legislators for their leadership. For the press, a Congress that defers to the president in a crisis and appears to avoid adopting a politically difficult position is not fulfilling its constitutional role.

NOTES

1. "The Carter Presidency," *New York Times*, November 7, 1976, p. E16.

2. Tom Wicker, "Mr. Carter's Mandate," *New York Times*, November 7, 1976, p. E17.

3. "Will Congress Seize Reins from a Democratic White House?" *U.S. News and World Report*, November 15, 1976, p. 25.

4. "What to Expect When Congress 'Welcomes' Carter," *U.S. News and World Report*, November 29, 1976, pp. 17–18.

5. "Carter's Record as Governor—Clues to the Future," *U.S. News and World Report*, December 13, 1976, p. 28. See also "Outlook-77: How Lawmakers Will Treat Ambitious White House Ideas," *U.S. News and World Report*, January 3, 1977, pp. 17–19; "A New Era Begins," *U.S. News and World Report*, January 24, 1977, p. 16.

6. Stanley Cloud, "Jimmy's Mixed Signals," *Time*, October 4, 1976, p. 30; "A Carter Administration," *Time*, November 8, 1976, pp. 24, 26; "Carter!" *Time*, November 15, 1976, p. 15; "Man of the Year," *Time*, January 3, 1977, p. 14; David Broder, "Carter's Dilemma," *Washington Post*, November 28, 1976, p. B7; Albert Hunt, "President Carter and Capitol Hill," *Wall Street Journal*, January 24, 1977, p. 16; "Enter Majority Rule," *New York Times*, January 3, 1977, p. 20; Anthony Lewis, "The Long and the Short," *New York Times*, March 3, 1977, p. A33.

7. "The Congress That Startled Everybody," *U.S. News and World Report*, December 19, 1977, p. 14.

8. "Outlook '78—In Congress, the Mood Will Get Even Feistier," *U.S. News and World Report*, January 2, 1978, p. 33.

9. Mark J. Rozell, *The Press and the Carter Presidency* (Boulder, CO: Westview, 1989), pp. 46–56. One article by David Broder stands out as an exception to the conventional wisdom that Congress needed strong presidential leadership to work effectively:

> Much has been said, most of it critical, of President Carter's handling of Congress. Less has been said—and more is justified—about Congress's handling of the president. The end-of-the-session assessments proceed on the assumption that in the circus that is Washington, Congress is the lion act and the president's job, as lion tamer, is to turn those brawling "cats" into a disciplined troupe of performers. This year, that analogy is . . . in error . . . because these "cats" in Congress have become increasingly immune to whip cracking.

David Broder, "The Senate Has No Excuse," *Washington Post*, December 18, 1977, p. C7. See also David Broder, "Tensions between Carter and Congress," *Washington Post*, March 2, 1977, p. A19.

10. Albert R. Hunt, "President Carter and Capitol Hill," *Wall Street Journal*, January 24, 1977, p. 16. See also Hedrick Smith, "Carter's Support in Congress, " *New York Times*, June 18, 1977, p. 7.

11. Albert R. Hunt, "Jimmy Carter vs. Congress," *Wall Street Journal*, March 25, 1977, p. 14.

12. John Herbers, "The Carter-Congress Rift May Just Have Started," *New York Times*, March 27, 1977, sec. 4, p. 4.

13. "On a Collision Course," *U.S. News and World Report*, April 18, 1977, p. 14.

14. Gerald Parshall, "Congress vs. President: Behind the Growing Feud," *U.S. News and World Report*, May 23, 1977, p. 23.

15. Lou Cannon, "The Independent Democrats," *Washington Post*, May 23, 1977, p. A6.

16. Edward Walsh, "Carter Has Mixed Scorecard in Skirmishes with Hill," *Washington Post*, June 19, 1977, p. A14. See also Adam Clymer, "One Party Rules, But Two Share the Power," *New York Times*, June 12, 1977, sec. 4, p. 2.

17. Joseph Kraft, "A Carter Base in the Congress?" *Washington Post*, June 19, 1977, p. B7.

18. Susan Fraker, "Shadowboxing," *Newsweek*, June 6, 1977, p. 15.

19. Thomas J. Foley, "Worst Congress in Years—Or Is It?" *U.S. News and World Report*, September 26, 1977, p. 26. See also Martin Tolchin, "Power Balance Tips to Congress from President," *New York Times*, October 9, 1977, p. 31.

20. "Carter and Congress," *U.S. News and World Report*, November 21, 1977, p. 21.

21. "Congress: Showdown Ahead," *Time*, November 7, 1977, p. 19.

22. Meg Greenfield, "The Club," *Newsweek*, October 10, 1977, p. 118.

23. Joseph Kraft, "Leadership by Reform," *Washington Post*, October 6, 1977, p. A19.

24. "They Are Paying the Price of Virtue," *Time*, March 14, 1977, p. 12. This news story noted that a Harris survey of public attitudes toward ten national institutions showed that members of Congress ranked eighth, only above corporation executives and labor bosses.

25. Foley, "Worst Congress in Years—Or Is It?" pp. 25–26.

26. "Income and Ethics on Capitol Hill," *Washington Post*, February 8, 1977, p. A18; "The Pay Raise Issue Persists," *Washington Post*, May 2, 1977, p. A22; "The Pay Raise in the House," *Washington Post*, June 28, 1977, p. A18; "On Ethics: Let the Third Shoe Drop," *New York Times*, February 20, 1977, sec. 4, p. 14; "At $57,500, It's Not a Poor House," *New York Times*, March 2, 1977, p. 20.

27. Marvin Stone, "Same Old Gang?" *U.S. News and World Report*, March 14, 1977, p. 88.

28. "Taking the Sugar without the Pill," *Washington Post*, February 6, 1977, p. C4.

29. "Make Me Take It," *Wall Street Journal*, February 4, 1977, p. 8. The *Journal* pointed out that members of Congress profit financially in many ways from their positions, including large capital gains on home appreciation in the District of Columbia metropolitan area. See "The Most Expensive Loophole," *Wall Street Journal*, March 21, 1977, p. 18.

30. Charles O. Jones, "Ronald Reagan and the U.S. Congress: Visible Hand Politics," in Charles O. Jones, ed., *The Reagan Legacy: Promise and Performance* (Chatham, NJ: Chatham House, 1988), p. 39.

31. "Where Are the Democrats?" *New York Times*, February 12, 1981, p. A26. See also Joseph Kraft, "The 'Republicrat' Debate," *Washington Post*, April 12, 1981, p. D7.

32. "Congress and the Reagan Cannonball," *New York Times*, March 22, 1981, sec. 4, p. 18. See also "The Reagan Road to Recovery," *New York Times*, February 22, 1981, sec. 4, p. 18; Martin Tolchin, "Moving on the Fast Track," *New York Times*, February 24, 1981, sec. 2, p. 10.

33. "Riding the Congressional Horse," *New York Times*, June 21, 1981, sec. 4, p. 22. See also "Behind the Battle," *Time*, December 7, 1981, p. 35.

34. "Crocodile Tears," *Wall Street Journal*, June 30, 1981, p. 30.

35. "Calling a Halt," *Wall Street Journal*, November 24, 1981, p. 32.

36. David S. Broder, "Congress Has No King," *Washington Post*, September 16, 1981, p. A25.

37. Hobart Rowen, "Tough to Buck Popular President," *Washington Post*, May 3, 1981, p. G7.

38. Haynes Johnson, "About This Matter of Summoning Spirits from the Vasty Deep," *Washington Post*, August 2, 1981, p. A3.

39. George F. Will, "A Day to Remember," *Newsweek*, July 6, 1981, p. 98.

40. Martin Tolchin, "Democrats Still Defensive, Hope to Generate an Offense," *New York Times*, March 29, 1981, sec. 4, p. 3. See also Mark Shields, "It's Okay to Act Like the Opposition," *Washington Post*, May 8, 1981, p. A19.

41. "The Coming Budget Showdown," *Washington Post*, December 10, 1981, p. A30.

42. Steven V. Roberts, "Budget Battle: Reagan Ahead," *New York Times*, February 11, 1981, p. 28.

43. "Congressional Cop-Out," *Wall Street Journal*, September 25, 1981, p. 32.

44. David Broder, "Have Pity on These Wretches," *Washington Post*, December 16, 1981, p. A31. See also "Christmastime on Capitol Hill," *Time*, July 27, 1981, p. 118.

45. "The Treason of Congress," *Wall Street Journal*, October 15, 1981, p. 28. See also "Tip's Gauntlet," *Wall Street Journal*, October 29, 1981, p. 30.

46. Rowland Evans and Robert Novak, "Tax Reform—Or Sausage?" *Washington Post*, April 18, 1986, p. A21.

47. "Tax Reform en Route to a Rout," *New York Times*, April 20, 1986, sec. 4, p. 24.

48. "Merry Christmas, Senator Packwood," *New York Times*, April 13, 1986, sec. 4, p. 24. See also David E. Rosenbaum, "Tax Bill: Leadership at Issue," *New York Times*, April 24, 1986, pp. D1, D2.

49. "After the Train Wreck," *Washington Post*, April 22, 1986, p. A14.

50. "A Tax Triumph for All Americans," *New York Times*, May 8, 1986, p. A26.

51. "Mr. Packwood's Amazing Tax Bill," *Washington Post*, May 8, 1986, p. A24. See also David Broder, " 'A Committee Has Redeemed Itself,' " *Washington Post*, May 11, 1986, p. D8.

52. Terry E. Johnson, "The Politics of Tax Reform," *Newsweek*, June 30, 1986, p. 24.

53. "Tax Reform: Last Lap, or Last Legs?" *New York Times*, August 8, 1986, p. A26.

54. E. J. Dionne, Jr., "For Richer, for Poorer, in Taxes and Ideology," *New York Times*, August 22, 1986, p. A10.

55. David E. Rosenbaum, "Congress's Mind Is Still Made Up," *New York Times*, September 14, 1986, sec. 4, p. 5.

56. Quoted in Gloria Borger, "A Legislative Super Bowl," *Newsweek*, July 21, 1986, p. 21.

57. Tom Wicker, "Who Gets the Credit?" *New York Times*, July 1, 1986, p. A23.

58. "Tax Transformation," *New York Times*, August 19, 1986, p. A26.

59. "A Tax Law to Hail. Yes, a Tax Law," *New York Times*, October 22, 1986, p. A30.

60. David S. Broder, "Give Reagan His Due—On Tax Reform *and* the Budget," *Washington Post*, August 20, 1986, p. A19. A *Time* cover story in August praised the congressional leadership for its accomplishment. See Dale Russakoff, "Weary Road to New Code," *Washington Post*, August 17, 1986, pp. A1, A8.

61. Gerald M. Boyd, "Claiming the Credit in 1988," *New York Times*, October 23, 1986, p. D18.

62. Steven V. Roberts, "How Tax Bill Breezed Past, Despite Wide Doubts," *New York Times*, September 26, 1986, p. A20.

63. "A Tax Law to Hail. Yes, a Tax Law," p. A30.

64. "An Army of Snipers vs. Fair Taxes," *New York Times*, September 19, 1986, p. A34.

65. "The Tax-Reform Rollback," *Wall Street Journal*, October 23, 1986, p. 32. See the even more critical George F. Will, " 'You Can't Argue with Success,' " *Washington Post*, September 25, 1986, p. A25.

66. "Congress Flunks Out On Deficit," *U.S. News and World Report*, November 10, 1986, p. 98.

67. "The Independent Counsel's Task," *Washington Post*, December 14, 1986, p. H6. See also "Iran 2: How Best to Find It Out," *New York Times*, December 14, 1986, sec. 4, p. 22.

68. Tom Wicker, "Mr. Reagan's Choice," *New York Times*, January 9, 1987, p. A27.

69. Tom Wicker, "Two Different Gates," *New York Times*, December 12, 1986, p. A35. See also Russell Baker, "Such a Swell Gang," *New York Times*, December 13, 1986, sec. 1, p. 27.

70. Linda Greenhouse, "Political Erosion: With a Shift of Gravity, Congress Begins Era," *New York Times*, January 4, 1987, sec. 4, p. 1.

71. Steven V. Roberts, "Congress Stands Ready to Test the Executive," *New York Times*, December 21, 1986, sec. 4, p. 1.

72. Norman Podhoretz, "The Imperial Congress," *Washington Post*, December 23, 1986, p. A19.

73. James J. Kilpatrick, "An Inefficient Engine Starts Again," *Washington Post*, January 4, 1987, p. C8.

74. Suzanne Garment, "We Don't Want Watergate Again, But Get It Anyway," *Wall Street Journal*, December 12, 1986, p. 28.

75. George F. Will, "Stonewalling on Immunity," *Washington Post*, December 17, 1986, p. A27.

76. "The Tower Report," *Wall Street Journal*, February 27, 1987, p. 14.

77. "The President's Speech," *Wall Street Journal*, March 4, 1987, p. 30.

78. "Reagan's Obligation," *Wall Street Journal*, May 5, 1987, p. 36.

79. "Not Following the Script," *Wall Street Journal*, May 12, 1987, p. 32.

80. Dan Morgan and Walter Pincus, "On Tuesday, Congress Raises Curtain on Iran-Contra Affair," *Washington Post*, May 3, 1987, pp. A1, A16.

81. Charles Krauthammer, "Spectacle," *Washington Post*, May 22, 1987, p. A27.

82. Linda Greenhouse, "As the Inquiry Unfolds, Pitfalls for Lawmakers," *New York Times*, July 21, 1987, p. A6.

83. See the criticisms by Norman Podhoretz, George F. Will, James J. Kilpatrick, and the *Wall Street Journal* editors noted earlier. See also R. Emmett Tyrrell, Jr., "Borne Aloft on Hot Air," *Washington Post*, July 21, 1987, p. A21.

84. Mary McGrory, "Congress and the Constitution," *Washington Post*, June 14, 1987, pp. H1, H5.

85. Mary McGrory, "The Congressional Equation," *Washington Post*, June 23, 1987, p. A2. See also Mary McGrory, "Who'll Break the Colonel's Spell?" *Washington Post*, July 12, 1987, pp. C1, C5.

86. David Ignatius, "Ollie's Last Laugh," *Washington Post*, July 12, 1987, pp. C1, C2.

87. Meg Greenfield, "Giving Truth a Bad Name," *Newsweek*, July 27, 1987, p. 64.

88. James Reston, "We Need an Election," *New York Times*, July 15, 1987, p. A27.

89. Tamar Jacoby, Robert B. Cullen, and Eleanor Clift, "Who's In Charge Here?" *Newsweek*, July 27, 1987, p. 18.

90. Haynes Johnson, "The Power Conflict in Iran-Contra Affair," *Washington Post*, May 31, 1987, pp. A4, A5.

91. Haynes Johnson, "The Healing Light of Disclosure," *Washington Post*, July 15, 1987, p. A2. See also Albert R. Hunt, "Beyond the Ollie Show," *Wall Street Journal*, July 15, 1987, p. 28.

92. Haynes Johnson, "Three Months of Hearings Fail to Crack the Case," *Washington Post*, August 4, 1987, pp. A1, A7.

93. "To Stop Elected Dictatorships," *New York Times*, August 9, 1987, sec. 4, p. 24. See also "The Iran-Contra Report," *Washington Post*, November 19, 1987, p. A22.

94. "The Iran-Contra Report," *Wall Street Journal*, November 20, 1987, p. 28.

95. "Reagan's Hard Lesson," *Wall Street Journal*, November 18, 1987, p. 32.

96. "High Noon for the Constitution," *Wall Street Journal*, July 14, 1987, p. 32. See also Raymond Price, "Were the Iran-Contra Hearings Worth It?" *Wall Street Journal*, August 7, 1987, p. 20.

97. Brian Duffy, "Who's In Charge Here?" *U.S. News and World Report*, November 24, 1986, pp. 18–22.

98. Peter Cary, "Examining the Loose Ends in the Iran-Contra Affair," *U.S. News and World Report*, October 26, 1987, pp. 22–23.

99. Mortimer B. Zuckerman, "Implausible Deniability," *U.S. News and World Report*, August 3, 1987, p. 103. See also David Gergen, "Disease of Distrust," *U.S. News and World Report*, July 27, 1987, p. 103.

100. James Carney, "Are They Worth It?" *Time*, January 23, 1989, p. 13.

101. Hays Gorey, "The Games Congress Plays," *Time*, February 13, 1989, p. 38.

102. Walter Shapiro, "Government by the Timid," *Time*, February 20, 1989, p. 38.

103. Larry Martz, "Profiles in Courage," *Newsweek*, February 13, 1989, pp. 14–16. See also "Profiles in Courage," *Wall Street Journal*, February 8, 1989, p. A22.

104. Larry Reibstein, "Pay Raises via the Back Door," *Newsweek*, January 30, 1989, p. 34; Eleanor Clift, "Sneaking Through a Pay Raise," *Newsweek*, December 19, 1988, p. 37.

105. "Salaries: Those Who Sow and Those Who Reap," *U.S. News and World Report*, December 26, 1988/January 2, 1989, p. 14. See also Andy Plattner, "Lawmakers' Pay-Raise Blues," *U.S. News and World Report*, February 6, 1989, p. 28.

106. Colman McCarthy, "The Pay Raise Doesn't Play," *Washington Post*, January 8, 1989, p. F2.

107. Judy Mann, " 'Compromising' on a Whopper," *Washington Post*, February 3, 1989, p. C3.

108. Jack Anderson and Dale Van Atta, "Do Lawmakers Deserve a Pay Raise?" *Washington Post*, January 31, 1989, p. C18.

109. Charles Krauthammer, "Congressional Cowardice," *Washington Post*, January 6, 1989, p. A19.

110. Richard Cohen, "Want a Raise? Vote for It," *Washington Post*, January 27, 1989, p. A21.

111. David Broder, "Congress Should 'Just Say Yes,' " *Washington Post*, December 11, 1988, p. C7.

112. "Paying One Way or Another," *Wall Street Journal*, December 14, 1988, p. A18.

113. "Pay-Raise Follies," *Wall Street Journal*, February 7, 1989, p. A24. See also "Comp Package for Congress," *Wall Street Journal*, January 30, 1989, p. A14.

114. "Look Ma, No Fingerprints," *Washington Post*, December 19, 1988, p. A12. See also "What Exactly Is an Honorarium?" *Washington Post*, December 11, 1988, p. C6.

115. "Congress: No One Home?" *Washington Post*, January 8, 1989, p. C6.

116. "A Phantom Steamroller," *Washington Post*, January 30, 1989, p. A8. See also "Mr. Wright Comes Home on Pay," *Washington Post*, February 7, 1989, p. A24; "Rabbit Holes," *Washington Post*, February 3, 1989, p. A24.

117. "The Costs of a Cowardly Congress," *New York Times*, February 8, 1989, p. A26. See also "Government by Black Boxes," *New York Times*, February 13, 1989, p. A20; "How to Pay for Honest Government," *New York Times*, February 1, 1989, p. A24; "Unfinished Business on Federal Pay," *New York Times*, February 27, 1989, p. A18.

118. "Pay the Price of Good Government," *New York Times*, December 14, 1988, p. A30. See also "The Cost of an Honest Congress," *New York Times*, January 14, 1989, p. 24; "Pay Congress for Service, Not Lunch," *New York Times*, August 1, 1988, p. A14.

119. Michael R. Kagay, "82 Percent in Poll Oppose the Congressional Raise," *New York Times*, February 6, 1989, p. A12.

120. The House vote was 380 to 48 and the Senate vote 94 to 6.

121. David Broder, "The Pay Raise Fiasco: Everybody Lost," *Washington Post*, February 12, 1989, p. C7.

122. Tom Kenworthy and Helen Dewar, "Divided Congress Grants President Authority to Wage War against Iraq," *Washington Post*, January 13, 1991, pp. A1, A25; Richard Lacayo, "A Reluctant Go-Ahead," *Time*, January 21, 1991, pp. 32–33.

123. Anthony Lewis, "War in the Gulf?" *New York Times*, October 22, 1990, p. A19.

124. Anthony Lewis, "War and the President," *New York Times*, November 30, 1990, p. A33.

125. George F. Will, "Mobilization's Deadly Momentum," *Washington Post*, November 15, 1990, p. A25.

126. George F. Will, "Better 60–40 Than No Vote at All," *Washington Post*, January 9, 1991, p. A19.

127. George F. Will, "Once Again, Ike Was Right," *Newsweek*, January 14, 1991, p. 60.

128. Charles Krauthammer, "Make Congress Choose," *Washington Post*, November 30, 1990, p. A29.

129. Charles Krauthammer, "An Executive Declaration of War," *Washington Post*, November 16, 1990, p. A19. See also Susan F. Rasky, "Congress Asks What It Should Do in the Gulf, and How," *New York Times*, November 18, 1990, sec. 4, pp. 1–2; Susan F. Rasky, "Congress and the Gulf," *New York Times*, December 17, 1990, pp. A1, A13; Adam Clymer, "102d Congress Opens, Troubled on Gulf But without a Consensus," *New York Times*, January 4, 1991, pp. A1, A8.

130. Nathaniel C. Nash, "Congress and the Crisis: To Intervene or Not?" *New York Times*, September 13, 1990, p. A10.

131. Mary McGrory, "The Hill's Own Wimp Factor," *Washington Post*, January 6, 1991, pp. C1, C5.

132. Mary McGrory, "Baker's Tempering Touch," *Washington Post*, November 15, 1990, p. A2.

133. "U.N. Logic," *Washington Post*, November 29, 1990, p. A22. See also "The 60–Day Clock," *Washington Post*, October 9, 1990, p. A20; "Making Timely Notice Timely," *Washington Post*, October 29, 1990, p. A14.

134. "The Gulf Buildup," *Washington Post*, November 11, 1990, p. B6. See also "Calling Back Congress," *Washington Post*, November 14, 1990, p. A16.

135. "War by Default," *New York Times*, December 16, 1990, sec. 4, p. 14.

136. "Who Can Declare War?" *New York Times*, December 15, 1990, p. A26.

137. "Where Is Congress on the Gulf?" *New York Times*, January 3, 1991, p. A20.

138. "Congress's Calhoun Strategy," *New York Times*, January 7, 1991, p. A16.

139. "Saddam's Protectors," *Wall Street Journal*, January 11, 1991, p. A10.

140. Paul A. Gigot, "No Bipartisanship from Congress in the Gulf," *Wall Street Journal*, November 16, 1990, p. A14. See also Paul A. Gigot, "As War Nears, Democrats Wiggle and Wobble," *Wall Street Journal*, January 11, 1991, p. A10.

141. George J. Church, "The Case for War," *Time*, November 26, 1990, p. 106.

142. See, for example, Anna Quindlen, "Consent of Congress," *New York Times*, December 6, 1990, p. A27; Tom Wicker, "Bush's War Powers," *New York Times*, November 18, 1990, sec. 4, p. 17; Tom Wicker, "Bush Stands Warned," *New York Times*, December 2, 1990, sec. 4, p. 19.

143. Robin Toner, "Mindful of History, Congress Agonizes over Going to War," *New York Times*, January 13, 1991, sec. 1, p. 12.

144. "Plan Now for Peace," *New York Times*, February 11, 1991, p. A18.

145. Anthony Lewis, "Presidential Power," *New York Times*, January 14, 1991, p. A17.

146. E. J. Dionne, Jr., "Foolishness Falls Victim to War Debate As Eloquence Escalates," *Washington Post*, January 12, 1991, pp. A8, A13. See also Adam Clymer, "Congress in Step," *New York Times*, January 14, 1991, p. A11.

147. David S. Broder, "Bravo, Congress," *Washington Post*, January 15, 1991, p. A21. See also David Broder, "Undervalued Congress," *Washington Post*, January 30, 1991, p. A21.

Chapter Five

The Era of Cynicism II (1990s)

It is almost a cliché to refer to the 1990s as a hypercynical era. Confidence in public institutions and leaders is at an all-time low. People have lost faith not only in their government but also in the media, education, and even private industry. Despite all objective criteria to the contrary—Americans are healthier, living longer, and more prosperous than ever—the public remains convinced that better days have passed and the future is frightening.

The disjuncture between reality and public perceptions is so great that in early 1996 a *Newsweek* cover screamed "Cheer up America!" and subheaded "It's Not As Bad As You Think."[1] Judging from recent press coverage and public perceptions of Congress, representative government is at the root of what ails society.

CONGRESS UNDER SIEGE I (1991–1992)

By the early 1990s, Congress bashing had become a national pastime. An October 1991 *New York Times*/CBS News poll showed that only 27 percent of the public approved of the job that Congress was doing, while 57 percent disapproved. A large majority, 83 percent, said that members of the House of Representatives overdrew their House bank accounts "because they knew they could get away with it." Only 9 percent said that the members had overdrawn by mistake, and 58 percent said that the perquisites of office given to members of Congress were "unjustifiable."[2] A March 1992 *Washington Post*/ABC News poll found that 63 percent of respondents believed that members who had overdrawn House accounts had acted illegally, and 84 percent said that they had behaved unethically. Finally, 79 percent said that they were less likely to vote for a representative who had overdrawn his or her House bank account.[3]

Given the press coverage of Congress in 1991–1992, it is no wonder the public holds its national legislature in such low esteem. In a column conspicuous because it argued for more balanced coverage of Congress, David Broder laid responsibility for the prevailing public contempt at the feet of the media. He felt compelled to respond that, as the title of the column made clear, "yes, there are good people in Congress." Broder wrote that many journalists had practiced a form of prejudice "that makes it impossible for people even to recognize individual differences within the reviled group." He identified some "hard-working, principled and effective" members of Congress and concluded:

> Somehow, their efforts go largely uncelebrated in the press. It's easy to get on the best-seller list by writing of Congress as the "Parliament of Whores" or to jump aboard the term limits bandwagon, feeding popular prejudice in the process. It takes more courage and independence to challenge the notion that everyone in Congress is crooked or incompetent or both. . . . Where is the journalism that reminds people that it's just as wrong to say that politicians are all crooks as to pretend they are all saints?[4]

Sensational news stories about transgressions of varying degrees contributed to the disparaging coverage of Congress. One subject was the so-called Keating Five—senators accused of pressuring federal banking regulators on behalf of campaign contributor Charles Keating, head of the former Lincoln Savings and Loan. Another topic was abuse of perquisites. Rubbergate involved the revelation that members of the House of Representatives had frequently overdrawn their accounts at the House bank, and Lunchgate, the revelation that members of Congress had run up large, unpaid bills at the Capitol dining room. Other reports focused on free parking, franked mail, free medical care, and cut-rate barber shops. Reports also pointed out that Congress exempted itself from various laws that it imposed on others, including title VII of the Civil Rights Act, the Americans with Disabilities Act, and the minimum wage. Finally, the Clarence Thomas confirmation hearings brought a barrage of stories criticizing the Senate confirmation process.

The editorial pages of the prestige newspapers led much of the criticism. The *Wall Street Journal* suggested a movie about the Keating Five directed either by Martin Scorsese or Francis Ford Coppola because "both have a fine feel for depicting little groups of men who decide they'll live by their own rules. They'd catch the elaborate traditions of deference, the mystical loyalties built on common behavior, and the system's real rewards." The *Journal* maintained that during its investigations, Congress vilified people who break laws, but that for its own members it tolerated "all but the most crass kinds of influence-peddling and interference with regulators" as " 'constituent service.' "[5] Another *Journal* editorial decried Congress's "abuse of constituent service" and "lap-dog Ethics committees." It called for "a deeper re-evaluation of what the modern Congress has become" and then offered it:

> There is a cancer eating away at the health of Congress. It is the stupendous expansion of government itself. The incentives to corruption are inevitable in any system where huge sums of money in endless categories are controlled and distributed by politicians and bureaucrats. A quarter of the nation's wealth—$1.2 trillion—is now siphoned off to Washington. It is a utopia for middlemen, deal-makers and arrangers. . . . . Congress has become less of a deliberative body and more like a special-interest vending machine.[6]

The *Journal* also picked up the hue and cry on the House bank controversy, which it described as "Congress's BCCI, the Bank for Check-Kiting Congressional Incumbents."[7] Another editorial commented with some sarcasm, "This is of course the same House of Representatives whose Members have been howling for a regulatory jihad against the real banking industry. . . . Curiously, the only Americans to have such banking privileges are the same ones who consistently fail to balance the nation's checkbook."[8]

The *New York Times* also denounced Congress for alleged breaches of ethics. "Whoever coined the adage 'There's no free lunch' obviously didn't have the House of Representatives in mind."[9] The *Times* further mocked House members. "Representatives have given new meaning to the expression 'on the House,' bouncing checks in the House bank, ignoring bills from the House restaurant, getting House officials to fix their parking tickets. All over the country voters have been smelling self-indulgence." The *Times* lambasted the "haughty privilege" of House members and called for reforms that would "reduce members' unseemly reliance on favor-seekers and enhance competition from challengers."[10] The *Times* argued that to put to rest the controversy over "the House's bank" meant "holding publicly accountable those who mismanaged or abused the bank."[11] "For an angry public, the twin embarrassments of the bouncing bank and the delinquent diners are fresh reminders of the need to transform Congress's attitude toward ethical behavior. It's the same smug attitude that, among other things, perpetuates a discredited campaign finance system and permits lawmakers to accept free trips from powerful lobbies."[12]

In March 1992 alone, the *New York Times* featured four editorials on the House bank controversy. It declared that "the public has every right to feel betrayed by the spectacle of special privilege run amok. More important, the systematic abuses raise troubling doubts about the integrity and judgement of individual members."[13] Furthermore,

> Perks like the bank are galling because they reflect a self-indulgent legislature that is often sorely out of touch with the real world. . . . The bank did its best to keep House members happy, providing yet another example of how many members live in a cocoon, insulated from the pressures that make life miserable for many constituents.[14]

> Congress's problems go far beyond self-indulgent perks and shoddy housekeeping. Both houses stagger through self-imposed obstacle courses that interrupt and paralyze their capacity to legislate. The larger task before Congress is to change the way it does business.[15]

Among the changes that the *Times* suggested were reforms of the "campaign finance cesspool." The *Times* argued that "the relentless pursuit of favor-seeking money by members of Congress, and the special advantages this money bestows, shames the House more than all the bad checks combined."[16] The *Times* also called for reforms of the franking privilege or of "politicking at public expense. There's still far too much taxpayer-financed junk mail. And there's a higher price: reinforced cynicism about Congress."[17]

The *Times* also attacked the Senate for the Keating Five scandal. It suggested that members of the Senate Ethics Committee be dubbed "the Senate Six" for not taking strong action against the members accused of influence peddling. "That has made the committee a laughingstock even in Washington, awash in scandals over private piggy banks and other congressional perks."[18] A subsequent editorial referred to the Senate as "the Keating One Hundred" and explained:

> The mixed conclusion to the scandal brought to 100—the full Senate membership—the number of senators tainted by the exposure of wretched ethical standards and subservience to big money. The Sen-

ate's refusal to reform campaign financing haunted the disciplinary proceedings from the first. . . . Now the remaining senators can address the larger sin: a system of moneyed politics of which the Keating episode is merely the most recent scandal.[19]

The *Washington Post* appealed to a populist disposition among readers, asking them, wouldn't it be nice to be able to draw no-interest, no-fee loans at will with no repayment schedule?

Well, no federal- or state-regulated bank in America would let you get away with that. Not even family or close friends are likely to indulge that fantasy. The one exception is the House of Representatives. Membership there means treating yourself as if you are every inch a king.

Subsidized haircuts, fixed traffic tickets, a nice gym and year-round open season to take pot shots at any bureaucrat you want—they have all that plus the keys to the vault.[20]

News stories added to the overall press view of Congress as mired in scandal and in privilege. A *Wall Street Journal* editorial entitled "The Keating 535" noted that the Keating controversy "captures the essence of today's Congress — a lawmaking institution that often resembles a service institution built on political money."[21]

Inexorably the focus broadened to include attacks on political privilege and scandals in general. An October 1991 *Time* news story declared Washington, D.C., "perk city." In bold black letters the article screamed, "Wonder why Congress is so arrogant about bounced checks? Perhaps because its members are so used to the freebie life." The article featured several cartoonlike drawings of "freebies" and perks doled out to members of Congress. These included three-dollar car washes, five-dollar haircuts, free picture framing, free prescription drugs, special parking privileges, a House gym with a masseuse, and subsidized eating establishments, "ranging from simple cafeterias to opulent dining rooms with crystal chandeliers and black-tie waiters" serving filet mignon for less than eight dollars. The list was by no means exhaustive.

Members of Congress expect to be called Honorable, but their claim to that honorific is looking pretty flimsy. . . . What could be a better invitation to civil-disobedience revolt than watching lawmakers who earn $125,100 travel around the world for free, have massages in the

House gym for free, have their cars parked for free and have their tickets fixed, refusing to pay for the few perks that are not granted outright?[22]

The article lambasted Congress for exempting itself from affirmative-action laws and the Freedom of Information Act.[23] It intoned that "this culture of privilege, so stubbornly protected, is not well suited to these hard times." Furthermore,

When uninsured workers live in fear that one illness could wipe out their life savings, it is enraging to hear of the House pharmacy dispensing free prescription drugs, not to mention the private congressional ambulance that protects members from the urban nightmare of emergency-room gridlock. When families who know how to squeeze a dollar until the eagle screams still cannot find the money for a haircut, the House barber takes on a special symbolic weight. When young families cannot get a mortgage on a house, the idea of free loans to lawmakers is bound to rankle.[24]

The following issue of *Time* decried Senate members as "pampered denizens of a virtually all-male bastion" and accused the upper chamber of institutionalized sexism:

When the Senate is not operating like a men's club, it behaves like a family—a patriarchal, dysfunctional family. Not only does the Senate have all the institutionalized forms of sexism common in the corporate suite, but by dint of its privileges and power it is one of the few places where acting like a cross between a rock star and the dictator of a banana republic is tolerated.[25]

The accoutrements of the Senate's pampered lifestyle included "offices [resembling] living rooms," leather furnishings, fourteen dining rooms, a gym with a sauna and steam room, and a pool. Furthermore, the Senate operated by arcane rules, "often unwritten, [that] demand a lifetime of male bonding to understand."[26]

Such word pictures were complemented by a resort to cartoons. A *Newsweek* story on the bank overdrafts and unpaid restaurant bills carried a drawing of startled congressmen sitting down to eat in a Capitol Hill restaurant and being served stacks of unpaid bills by the waiters. The story noted that if the congressmen "had set out on purpose to demonstrate arrogance of office and contempt for the rules that bind ordinary mortals, they couldn't have done better."[27] A *U.S. News* report carried a drawing of rats, clothes stuffed with cash, bouncing rubber checks off the Capitol. The report declared that "the bank mess simply confirmed the institutional arrogance that makes all members politically suspect."[28] In another cartoon accompanying a *U.S. News* story about the "rubber barons" on Capitol Hill, a woman proclaimed, "I just saw our Congressman on T.V." "Not another campaign ad," her husband complained. "No. 'America's Most Wanted,' " the woman answered. A disapproving child fired his slingshot at the television screen.[29]

After the House decided in a postmidnight vote to reveal the names of members who had overdrawn their accounts, a *Washington Post* news story sarcastically asked, "Is Congress naturally nocturnal?" Recalling the much-maligned Senate "midnight pay raise" vote of a 'year earlier—a vote that actually took place before 10:00 P.M.—the article asked, "Why do members of the House and Senate seem incapable of making the big decisions, particularly big decisions about themselves, during daylight? Are their circadian rhythms different from ours, or is the perception that Congress does things in the dead of night to avoid scrutiny actually a misperception?"[30]

Another *Post* report described Congress as plagued by "scandals worthy of Peyton Place." Congress was "coasting along on its inertia, ripe for abuse and mired in an 'I'm all right, Jack' mentality that assumed that somehow, somewhere, there was someone that knew what was going on."[31]

The nation's best-known columnists also contributed to the poor image of Congress. David Gergen, then *U.S. News* editor-at-large, acknowledged that "there are far fewer drunks, crooks and scalawags roaming the halls" of Congress than twenty years ago. Nonetheless, "Money from special-interest groups slashes through Washington, buying votes and blocking progress." Gergen accused the Congress of "acting like a House of Lords" because of the various perquisites enjoyed by members:

How can Congress justify having its own pharmacy that dispenses free medicine, an ambulance service for members only and a system that tears up parking tickets? How does it explain a congressional retirement plan that pays out two to three times as much as most private pensions? . . . The arrogance of Congress is most vividly on display when it passes major legislation, proclaiming on television that it is saving the country from some horrid practice, but quietly exempts itself from the law's operation.[32]

George F. Will has been one of the most vocal advocates of term limits for members of Congress. Calling limits "an auxiliary precaution against the perennial lust for power," Will accused Congress of "degrading itself by undisciplined wallowing in inessentials." He characterized Congress as overly solicitous of pressure groups, trying to do too much for them while failing to do its important duties.[33] In another column, Will referred to term limits as "antitrust policy in politics," or an attempt to "regulate competition in order to intensify it." The "seasoned professionals" in Congress had created huge deficits, were mired in scandal, and had failed to deal effectively with the nation's policy problems. "Do you think 'amateurs' would do worse?" Will added,

> Stung by criticism—of its profligacy, its perquisites, its transformation of government into an incumbents protection machine—and terrified of term limits, Congress has reformed. The House of Representatives' barber shop is doubling the price of its taxpayer-subsidized haircuts. Why does Congress need barbers? Presumably legislators are so important and so busy, busy, busy doing urgent work, they must economize every minute.[34]

Rowland Evans and Robert Novak believed that public anger at Congress was widespread because it "arrogates special privileges unto itself, raises its pay in the dead of night, conspires with state legislators to keep districts noncompetitive and presides over rising government spending."[35] *Time* columnist Michael Kramer asked in an essay entitled "Shame on Them All," whether Congress would "finally get with the program and have its workplace governed by the laws that apply in the rest of the nation?"[36] He offered the following view:

> No legislature is more entrenched and more dynastic than the one in Washington. Congress has become a ruling elite insulated from accountability to all but the interests who spend lavishly to win its attention. Attempts to level the playing field—for example, by instituting campaign finance reform laws that would even the odds of a challenger's unseating an incumbent—have been regularly gutted. If real reform is beyond the capacity of Congress to fashion, the only option left is to kick the members out.[37]

In its 1992 "Man of the Year" issue, *Time* featured a harsh critique by Stanley Cloud entitled "Bums of the Year." He opened as follows: "Like fish in a barrel, Congress has always been too good a target to miss. From the very beginning, the tendency of the nation's lawmakers to posture or steal or make damn fools of themselves has been an inspiration to reformers and parodists alike." Cloud characterized Congress as full of "so much arrogance, so much corruption, so much abuse of the system." Furthermore, "Congress remains more concerned with protecting itself and its prerogatives than with helping solve the nation's manifold domestic problems." He posed the problem with rhetorical questions:

What's to be said in defense of an institution that prates endlessly about equal opportunity, fair employment, and freedom of information, then excludes itself from most of the laws that would help achieve those goals? How can there be anything but contempt for politicians who decry the projected $365 billion federal deficit even as they pour more and more dollars into their pet programs? Is there a case for the Keating Five and the way those purblind Senators opened their doors to convicted savings and loan rip-off artist Charles Keating—not to mention the purblind way in which the Senate ethics committee investigated the offense?

Only a chronic rubber-check artist, after all, is likely to applaud the sweetheart deal Congress cut for itself with its own private bank. And only sophists are likely to go along with the argument that accepting bundles of money from political-action committees is not tantamount to taking bribes. Congress's refusal to consider real reform of its campaign-finance system makes sense only to other professional politicians, for many of whom retention of power is the paramount goal.[38]

Tom Kenworthy, who covered Congress for five years for the *Washington Post*, declared that perhaps it was time for voters to send a message to Congress by defeating incumbents. In his view, many members of Congress were "buffoons, charlatans, blowhards and intellectually dishonest people." But with all of the criticism of the national legislature, "Perhaps a little Congress-defending is in order. Not much, mind you, but if [mass murderer] Jeffrey Dahmer deserves a defense, then Congress does too." Kenworthy sarcastically added that indeed, Congress was paralyzed, incapable of enacting meaningful public policy or campaign-finance reform, too wedded to special interests. "But all of that has very little, if anything, to do with parking spaces or the House gym or free allergy medication at the office of the attending physician. Or kiting checks."[39]

Haynes Johnson identified "a dual standard practiced by politicians here—a standard that holds it's all right for members to bounce checks and run up big restaurant tabs without paying for them but wrong for anybody else who gets caught in such mistakes or finagling." He stated that the symbolic importance of the bank overdrafts was substantial, particularly when placed alongside "disclosures about congressional deadbeat practices for meals and catering services," and that Americans have a good understanding of what happens to them when they overdraw their bank accounts. "The House bank covered the checks and did not exact penalties from the offenders. Try that at your friendly neighborhood bank, Mr. and Mrs. American Citizen, and see how far you'll get. And this, mind you, comes at a time of great economic distress and anxiety nationwide."[40]

Finally, the darkest reading of Congress's transgressions came from Mary McGrory, who contended that Congress could not effectively challenge the power of the president. Because of the "proliferating lists of sinners," she wrote, the legislature was "incapacitated," unable to confront serious national problems. Suddenly, a good many congressmen decided to call it quits. "People who were at least in a position to do something about the staggering problems that face us have thrown up their hands. What are the rest of us, who have no power, supposed to do? Is it any wonder that the turnout in the [presidential] primaries is so low? What good is government anyway?"[41]

William Safire asserted that the congressional franking privilege constituted the "most egregious example of nest-feathering" in the nation's legislature. "This enables incumbents to advertise with self-serving, junk-mail newsletters and 'meeting notifications' at a cost to the public of tens of millions each year."[42] Paul Gigot noted that because of public anger at Congress, "members are quivering along with their kited checks."[43] Meg Greenfield wrote that despite congressional reforms of the financing laws, congressmen "have ended up as much as ever in thrall to special interests, so new reforms of the reforms are desperately needed." She described Congress as mired in "indiscipline verging on chaos."[44]

Despite his earlier column extolling the need to emphasize that Congress has many good, professional people, David Broder joined the chorus of criticism. Congress had become "a personal plaything for its members." He noted the symbolic importance of the overdrawn bank accounts and described the Congress as indulged in self-serving pursuits:

The bank was in the Capitol building, which both symbolically and legally belongs to the nation and all its citizens. The clowns who ran it were on the federal payroll, supported by our taxes. . . . That pattern—of individual self-interest prevailing over collective responsibility—is what's wrong with Congress. . . . Far too many of today's House members are individual entrepreneurs, in political business for themselves, and they have made the House a place that is run—like the defunct bank—for the benefit and convenience of its individual members, not for any larger purpose.[45]

By the end of the 102d Congress, the press judged the institution's record, as Helen Dewar assessed, "one of the thinnest . . . within memory."[46] Gloria Borger reported that the "Congress that opened with a noble discourse on the Persian Gulf War skulked out of town."[47] A Harris poll in September asked respondents whether members of Congress possessed good moral and ethical standards. Only 19 percent said "yes," a lower rating than those given to business people, the Bush administration, journalists, and lawyers.[48]

The criticism of Congress in 1991–1992 was unrelenting. The press left the overwhelming impression of the institution as self-indulgent, scandal ridden, incompetent, and corrupt. A *New York Times*/CBS poll found that almost one-half of the public believed that members of Congress had used taxpayer money to cover the bank overdrafts, and two-thirds wrongly believed that the members had broken the law by overdrawing checks at the House bank.[49]

It is no surprise that the public held Congress in such extraordinarily low esteem when influential editorialists and columnists had nothing positive to say about the institution. The coverage and consequent public anger led many members to retire from public service.[50] One of them, Matthew McHugh (D–N.Y.), said that he had become tired of having to defend himself merely because he was a congressman. By March 1992, the *New York Times*/CBS poll showed that only 14 percent of registered voters approved of Congress's performance. In July 1992, the approval rating stood at only 18 percent.[51]

CONGRESS UNDER SIEGE II (1993–1995)

To many analysts, the 1992 elections results sent a clear message that the public was fed up with the federal government and wanted change. Congress was a target of the public anger, but so too was the incumbent president, George Bush. After the elections, with a new president and 110 new members of Congress, expectations for substantial political change ran high. One-party control of the political branches—after an extended period of divided government—contributed to the heightened expectations.

The performance of President Bill Clinton and the Democratic Congress throughout 1993 did not match the inflated public expectations. Although Clinton and Congress had some real policy achievements in such areas as deficit reduction and family/medical leave, the public remained impatient with the government's pace of initiative and reform. The president and many legislators complained of a hypercritical media that fueled public cynicism and failed to credit real accomplishment.

By 1994, when members returned to Washington for the second session of the 103d Congress, a *Washington Post* survey found the institution's approval rating at only 29 percent. Another survey revealed that 57 percent believed that lobbyists and special interests ran the government. The *Post* cited as reasons for such low public esteem the accusations of misconduct by two members, congressional junkets, lobbyist activities, and continuing investigations of the House Post Office controversy.[52]

Several months later, the *Post* detailed additional allegations of misconduct by members that it blamed for the low public esteem of Congress.[53] An editorial maintained "that Congress has developed a terrible reputation and that some considerable part of it reflects the reality of life there and is fair."[54]

More discouraging yet, in July, a *Post* poll found that Congress's approval rating was the lowest among the more well-informed citizens. That finding was contrary to the long-standing belief among congressionalists that public cynicism could be attributed in part to a lack of knowledge about the institution. The *Wall Street Journal* quipped: "No wonder congressional leaders are becoming increasingly hostile to C-SPAN."[55] Two months later, an Associated Press poll revealed that only 14 percent trusted Congress to do what is right most of the time. The *Journal* reacted that "a large measure of this cynicism is the consequence of Congress passing huge pieces of legislation . . . with no clear idea of the law's effects or costs in the real world."[56]

Negative coverage of Congress prevailed throughout 1994 and had an impact on the public disposition. For example, a February 21 *U.S. News* cover story pictured the Capitol next to the boldfaced headline "THE PORK BARREL BARONS." The investigative report purported to reveal "how an elite cadre of congressmen squanders your tax dollars."[57] In April, negative coverage centered on the Senate's vote to maintain free parking privileges for members at Washington, D.C., airports. The *Post* sarcastically editorialized: "It was tense, but the perk survived by a vote of 53 to 44. After all, these are special people, even in a democracy."[58]

In May and June, extensive coverage surrounded the trial and indictment of House Ways and Means Chairman Dan Rostenkowski (D–Ill.) on ethics charges—that he had used his high office for personal gain. George F. Will wrote that Rostenkowski was a symbol of the widespread practice of lawyers "renting" Washington politicians.[59] Reports suggested that Rostenkowski's plight furthered the image of members of Congress as having and exploiting special privileges not available to others.[60] In June, reports that members of Congress had substantially cut back on travel resulted in negative stories about the fact that the members still occasionally took junkets. Reports focused on certain members who took trips to exotic locations at the expense of lobbyists and private interests.[61]

By August, the *Post* had given a nod of approval to former Tennessee governor Lamar Alexander's call to cut the pay of members of Congress in half and send them home for one-half of the year. "Congress does operate in ways that seem cumbersome, labyrinthine, often nasty and ultimately incomprehensible to a lot of Americans. . . . Mr. Alexander's audiences seem to think that there just might be a better and no less democratic way for Congress to do its job. They may be right."[62]

Ultimately, the press concluded that the 103d Congress did not live up to the potential for single-party control of the political branches. Editorials and reports characterized the Democratic Congress as having failed for not enacting substantial environmental, health-care, housing, anticrime, education, and ethics legislation. The *Washington Post* led the criticism, lambasting the "dismal" performance of Congress and calling the 103d "perhaps the worst Congress—least effective, most destructive, nastiest—in 50 years." Furthermore, to the old adage that one should never watch sausage or legislation being made, "We are prepared to say that this adage is grossly unfair to sausage makers."[63] Corroborating the poor press reviews, a study of television news treatment of Congress released in September showed that negative stories about the institution outpaced positive ones by over a 2–1 margin.[64]

By October, the press was speculating about the possible electoral impact of the public's sour mood. Richard L. Berke reported on the results of focused interviews with citizens: people were "irritable," "dispirited," "cynical," "scared about their futures." They perceived incumbent politicians as corrupt and overpaid. Many said that they were ready, once again, for change.[65] Some members of Congress complained of the public's cynicism. Said one, "Voters are angry with politicians like me. . . . Well let me tell you something: The voters are no bargains either."[66]

The *New York Times* suggested that voters might react by electing a GOP Congress. The voters were disillusioned by presidential-congressional grid-lock under one-party control.[67] David S. Broder cited polling data to also show that Democrats in Congress could bear the electoral brunt of the voters' anger.[68]

Candidates both incumbent and challenger ran for Congress in 1994 by running against the institution. Although that is not unique, in 1994 the tone and imagery were unusually dark. Candidate advertisements pictured the Capitol dome as a symbol of greed and corruption. Some ads intoned that term limits were intended "to stop career politicians" as the death penalty was needed "to stop career criminals."[69] Senator Bob Kerrey ran ads calling government "the most formidable enemy of all."[70] Members of Congress were correct to lament the media cynicism that was undercutting support for representative government, but the members and their opponents had some responsibility for fueling cynical attitudes with negative advertise-ments. To Gerald F. Seib, incumbents were being "hypocritical."[71]

The *Wall Street Journal* editorial page led much of the criticism of Congress as a corrupt institution in need of fundamental change. Such *Journal* writers as John H. Fund contributed op-ed essays backing these charges. For example, Fund lambasted the "corruption, shoddy services and arrogance that have characterized [the] ruling elites."[72]

Of course, if voters opted for change, a Newt Gingrich–run GOP would benefit. Press interest surged with the prospect of Gingrich leading the 104th Congress. But the press portrait was no more flattering. Echoing the tone of many commentaries, *Time* described Gingrich as a "Republican carni-vore," "G.O.P. guerilla," and a "bomb-throwing" conservative. Like many others, *Time* recounted unflattering stories of Gingrich's first marriage, legislative record, and knowledge of the details of policy.[73] This report offered a foreshadowing of later press coverage and commentary.[74]

The Elections of 1994

With Gingrich's leadership, House GOP candidates orchestrated a re-markably unified national campaign in 1994. In September, the candidates unveiled their "Contract with America" on the Capitol steps. The GOP contract was a ten-point plan specifying the goals of a Republican-led Congress. The Republicans promised that if given a majority, they would act on all ten items—including term limits, a balanced budget amendment, and congressional reform—in the first hundred days of the 104th Congress.

The strategy paid off as election day saw the end of forty years of Democratic control of the House of Representatives. Representative Tom Foley (D–Wash.) became the first House Speaker to lose reelection since 1862. The GOP picked up 52 House seats and 8 in the Senate. The extent of its triumph surprised even the most optimistic GOP partisans. Not a single GOP incumbent in Congress lost.

The GOP tidal wave was an extraordinary story in itself. The rise of Gingrich to House Speaker made for even better copy, for he possesses qualities that the media are drawn to: he is colorful, controversial, and turns a good quotable phrase on command. To *Time* he was the "china-and-crystal smashing congressman."[75] Yet the *New York Times*, which had described Gingrich as a salesman who marketed "nostalgia and oversimplified remedies," acknowledged that "much of the House crystal that he has broken . . . needed breaking."[76] Specifically, the *Times* meant Gingrich's proposals to reform House committees and procedures.

Press reports emphasized that the 1994 elections results were not a referendum in favor of the GOP's Contract with America.[77] Indeed, a good many used polls to show that the public had little expectation for positive change in Congress and had voted incumbents out of office due to a generalized disgust with the institution. A *Time* poll reported that by a $3\frac{1}{2}$ –1 margin respondents expected more, rather than less, gridlock in Washington with a GOP Congress.[78] Furthermore, by a 2–1 margin, respondents expected the continuation of "politics as usual" instead of a "new era" of governance.[79] The GOP had so far failed to "convince voters that Republicans in Congress can move beyond heckling and obstructing to meet the public demand for leaner, more effective, more accountable government."[80]

A *New York Times* poll found that voters had not given a positive affirmation to conservative proposals. The voters instead had expressed disgust with "special interest groups and members of Congress from both parties."[81] The *Wall Street Journal* poll found that a majority perceived the elections results as a general preference for "change," 19 percent said they were a repudiation of Clinton, and only 12 percent said that they evidenced a desire for a more conservative Congress.[82] *Newsweek*'s poll noted that only half of the public had even heard of the Contract with America and that half of them dismissed it as mere campaign rhetoric.[83]

According to Gloria Borger, "Many voters weren't endorsing the GOP so much as they were demanding the change they thought they had voted for in 1992."[84] The *Washington Post* opined that voters had not only registered disapproval of President Clinton's leadership, they had acted "against Congress as well."[85] Furthermore, it was "disgust with the workings of Washington" that had much to do with the GOP ascent.[86] Citing Foley's defeat as the most telling symbol, the *Times* identified "voter discontent with congressional indulgence of the status quo" as a major factor.[87] Joe Klein agreed that voters had cast a negative vote against "public business as it has been performed."[88] *Newsweek* suggested that the GOP takeover occurred because of public anger at incumbents' use of perks.[89] Steven V. Roberts maintained that the elections did not prove that the public was eager for a sharp ideological change in government policy and a dismantling of the federal government.[90] Only the more conservative commentators perceived the results as an affirmation of increased voter conservatism.[91]

Press reports also emphasized the substantial gender gap in voting. In 1992, the press had extolled the "Year of the Woman." But 1994, according to the *Washington Post*, was the "Year of the Angry Man."[92] Fifty-four percent of men voted Republican in the congressional races; the same percentage of women voted Democratic. William Raspberry saw the elections results as "the revenge of the white guy," John Leo perceived a reaction against multiculturalism, and for Joe Klein they were a reaction against the excesses of legally protected ethnic groups and public-employee unions.[93]

Some expressed concern that the GOP takeover would deprive Congress of its historic collegiality—"everywhere the rhetoric is getting nastier," *Time* lamented—while others expressed little hope for a more productive Congress.[94] *Newsweek* went even further: "Americans . . . chose a Congress that looked and sounded like Rush Limbaugh."[95] According to Gloria Borger, "The bomb throwers have taken over the Old Boys' Club." Republicans for years had become "proficient with the wrecking ball." To effectively lead, they would need "reprogramming."[96] Defeated House Speaker Tom Foley explained in his final press conference that he and other Democrats had failed to communicate Congress's accomplishments. Furthermore, he said that Congress bashing by members of the institution had taken its toll and caused public cynicism.[97]

Journalists marveled at the historic significance of the party-composition change in Congress. Mortimer B. Zuckerman likened the GOP takeover to the Boston Tea Party.[98] Columnist Robert J. Samuelson called the change in Congress possibly "the most momentous since the mid-1960s" because of the likely end to the era of governmental expansion.[99] If the contract were enacted, according to *Newsweek*, it "would be the most significant reversal of direction by the United States government since the New Deal."[100]

Nonetheless, change in the partisan composition of Congress did little to end press cynicism and in many respects sharpened it. Some warned of

ominous consequences should the GOP succeed in enacting its contract.[101]
A *Newsweek* cover story claimed that GOP policies would end government
discretionary spending: "That means no FBI, no weather service, no coast
guard, no money for subways or highways or schools. The Republicans are
dodging this reality."[102] *Newsweek* also claimed that "the GOP wants to cut
your taxes and whack welfare. That may be more painful than it sounds."[103]
Time intoned that "a zealous crop of freshmen wants to yank the agenda
rightward. . . . They are the Jacobins in this revolution."[104] Steven V.
Roberts warned of the GOP's "harsh approach" to solving social problems.
He characterized the newly elected Republicans as "cultural counterrevo-
lutionaries" who did not recognize the inconsistencies in advocating less
government and social policy reforms.[105] Roberts also expressed skepticism that the Republicans who had "spent years stirring up anticongres-
sional fervor" could effectively reform an institution they had "helped to
discredit."[106]

The First Hundred Days

Although press treatment of the GOP Congress was largely negative
during this period, the institution received uncharacteristically extensive
and in-depth coverage. The major print sources periodically tracked the
GOP's progress during the first hundred days on the ten Contract items. The
Washington Post, for example, frequently featured "The Contract with
America: Scorecard" detailing House, Senate, conference committee, and
presidential action on each item. The *Wall Street Journal* also occasionally
featured a table "The GOP Contract with America" describing the status of
GOP legislation in the first hundred days.

The *Post*'s coverage of Capitol Hill during this period was the most
extensive. The paper featured an occasional in-depth series entitled "Changing the Guard." Series articles examined the changes taking place in
Congress under GOP leadership. The *Post* also featured a series of lengthy
articles called "Inside the Revolution." These articles took a close look
specifically at the activities of the new GOP majority. Finally, the *Post*'s
Federal Page presented a detailed ten-part series analyzing each of the GOP
Contract items.

On January 4, 1995, the first day of the 104th Congress, the House of
Representatives passed a number of reforms promised by the GOP leadership. These included more open committee meetings, streamlined committees, reduction in committee staff by one-third, elimination of certain
committees, term limits for the Speaker as well as committee and subcom-

mittee chairs, and a requirement that laws that apply to the private sector and the executive branch also apply to Congress. Sources as diverse as the *Post*'s Meg Greenfield and the editors of the *Wall Street Journal* praised the latter reform. According to the *Journal*: "If members are subject to the same out-of-control legal liability as other Americans, they may insist on more careful drafting of laws. Some members may even insist on reading laws before they vote for them. Imagine that."[107]

Many journalists also praised the new political dialogue in the nation's capital. The *Post*, although not enamored of the Contract, admitted that the GOP had "compelled reinspection of a number of programs and issues and ways of operating that were long overdue for such attention."[108] David S. Broder agreed that it was beneficial for leaders to be seriously debating fundamental issues such as federalism, the welfare state, and the size of government. "You can walk into almost any committee room on Capitol Hill and hear serious argument about the scope of the federal government."[109]

Early press reviews also signaled warnings for the GOP Congress. Broder implored the new leadership not to misunderstand its mandate and wrongly assume that the public hates everything that the federal government does.[110] The *Post* warned that the GOP leadership needed "to demonstrate that they aren't representing just the haves, aren't heedless of the problems of the have-nots."[111] The paper also predicted that despite promises to change the norms of Capitol Hill, Republicans would "be tempted to preserve arrangements that suit their purposes quite well."[112] Foreshadowing conservative criticism of the GOP leadership for not moving boldly enough to reform, Robert D. Novak criticized Gingrich for not promising immediately to eliminate "a flagrant congressional perquisite"—generous pensions for members of Congress.[113] On the fourth day of the new Congress, a *Post* news story based on interviews with Chicago-area voters revealed a sentiment "to provoke another upheaval on Capitol Hill two years from now if once again they are disappointed."[114]

Indeed, throughout the first hundred days, a number of reports and commentaries took the GOP Congress to task for not living up to the promise of fundamental reform. According to these assessments, the Senate was too wedded to the traditions of "filibusters and freebies" to change its ways;[115] members were not acting strongly enough to end perks;[116] lobbyists and PACs still held too much power in Congress;[117] and the GOP members did not sign on to support campaign-finance reform, presumably because they wanted the incumbency advantages that Democrats had enjoyed for so many years.[118] As Guy Gugliotta put it, "For Congress, currently emerging from the Stone Age," promoting progress is "a bit like advising Cro-Magnon man to forget the wheel and go directly to ball bearings."[119]

The failed reform efforts that received the most attention were the balanced-budget amendment and term limits. Most journalists considered these proposals dubious. Yet, as Broder and others pointed out with regard to the balanced-budget initiative—which failed in the Senate by one vote— these initiatives were based on unmistakable GOP campaign pledges. Failure to act on them affirmatively merely contributed to public cynicism. Many mocked the House Republicans in particular for failing to sufficiently back their own term-limits promise once in office. To Robert Novak, GOP leaders had "broken faith with voters."[120] The *Washington Post* summed up that sentiment: "The real question is why term-limits enthusiasts ever believed that these political pros would give them what they wanted."[121]

Other criticisms centered on the rhetoric of the new GOP leaders and freshman members. Some commented that GOP leaders occasionally resorted to inflammatory rhetoric and did not sufficiently respect the tradition of political decorum.[122] Furthermore, liberal commentators characterized the GOP programs as insensitive to the disadvantaged in society. As Mary McGrory wrote: "It tells you almost everything about the new Republican Congress that the poor, the left-out, the elderly and the very young are looking to the Senate, the hotbed of millionaires, lawyers and egotists, for rescue."[123]

Ironically perhaps, a good deal of press criticism centered on the GOP, in Charles Krauthammer's words, "doing too much too fast."[124] According to this view, despite years of criticism of Congress for acting too slowly and chaotically, GOP success at moving forward many of its other initiatives resulted in hastily drawn and often flawed legislation.[125] *Newsweek* speculated that the result of such fast action, like the War on Poverty, "will probably be a whole new batch of unintended consequences."[126] Robert J. Samuelson maintained that the GOP had "overreached" by promoting the "irresponsible" idea of balancing the budget with tax cuts.[127] David Broder wrote that because of resolute House GOP action, the country would have to look to the Senate for more deliberative, moderate action on legislation.[128]

A Center for Media and Public Affairs content analysis of press treatment of the Congress during March corroborated the finding of negative coverage. *New York Times* coverage of the Congress was negative 70 percent of the time. Almost as negative was the *Washington Post* (66 percent). The *Wall Street Journal* coverage was also predominantly negative (53 percent). The Center found that news and editorial coverage for each paper was very similar in negative tone.[129]

Despite all of this criticism, journalists credited the GOP leadership with having succeeded at changing the political dialogue in Washington during the first hundred days. According to the *Post*: "As with presidents, so it has been with them: The greatest power of those who occupy the national stage is to set the terms of the debate. They've done that."[130]

After One Hundred Days: The Rise of Gingrich Nation

The elite press maintained a tough stance toward the GOP Congress throughout the year. In part because of GOP campaign rhetoric promising fundamental reform, no more "politics as usual," even a "revolution," activities that smacked of status quo politics came under especially harsh journalistic fire. Like the Democratic majority before them, the Republicans had become enamored of pork-barrel projects.[131] Numerous reports and commentaries criticized the GOP Congress for welcoming lobbyist input into the legislative process. Despite pledges of change, the *Journal* reported, lobbyists remained "as powerful as ever—and perhaps more visible."[132] The GOP newcomers, according to the *Post*, were "would-be reformers."[133] Republicans said that they supported campaign-finance reform, but once in office, according to the *Times*, they began to like the system.[134] A *Post* "Inside the Revolution" article was especially critical: "From House Republicans come measures that gratify industry: weakening environmental standards, loosening workplace safety rules, limiting the legal liability of corporations, defunding nonprofit groups that present an opposing view. From the beneficiaries of that legislation come millions of dollars in campaign contributions."[135]

Some of the most critical commentary questioned the wisdom of GOP proposals and leadership of Congress. During prolonged and contentious budget negotiations with the president that led to two federal government shutdowns, the GOP received the brunt of press criticism for allegedly seeking to cut too deeply into government programs and not negotiating in good faith.[136] A *U.S. News* cover story on the budget battle featured mock pictures of the president and Gingrich hurling insults, with the Speaker's character screaming, "Liar, liar, pants on fire" and "My way, my way, or else." The inside story opened with a striking one-and-one-half-page photograph of two dejected tourists from Los Angeles just turned away from the Statue of Liberty because of a government shutdown.[137] Most of the negative coverage focused on Congress. During the second partial federal government shutdown, numerous reports and commentaries pointed out that legislators continued to receive pay while federal workers on furlough did not. A *Post* editorial-page writer blasted the "hypocritical and fully paid congressional elite [that] pleads penury to the nation's poor, takes taxpayer-paid vacations and makes plans to junket like mad around the world."[138] Opinion polls showed that the public overwhelmingly blamed the GOP-led Congress, not the president, for the government budget stalemates.[139]

Even those who acknowledged the need for fiscal austerity pointed out that the GOP proposals were not in the national interest.[140] Many did not accept the GOP assumptions in balanced-budget plans.[141] GOP tax-cut proposals were characterized as irresponsible "feel good actions."[142] Welfare-reform efforts allegedly were insensitive to the poor.[143] Commentators as diverse in viewpoint as Russell Baker, Mary McGrory, and David Gergen, among others, claimed that GOP plans, if enacted, would inflict enormous pain on the middle and underclass.[144] Journalists strongly criticized even the oversight activities by congressional committees investigating the Clintons' Whitewater investment and the government's disastrous raid of a religious sect's compound in Waco, Texas.[145] By the end of the year, the press concluded that the GOP revolution had fizzled. The *Post* declared it "long on promise, short on results." After all of the hoopla, journalists concluded, the GOP-led Congress had a meager record of achievement.[146]

Enormous coverage in 1995 also focused on the personal scandals and misdeeds of a few members. Most notable, a Senate ethics committee found credible evidence that Senator Bob Packwood (R–Oreg.) had misused his office by repeatedly engaging in sexual misconduct toward female staff and lobbyists; by soliciting financial support for his spouse from people with an interest in legislation; and by altering diary entries to cover up possible wrongdoing. Substantial press coverage focused on the allegations and Senate action that ultimately led to Packwood's resignation. Considerable coverage also attended the revelations of financial irregularities in first-term Representative Enid Waldholtz's (R–Utah) 1994 campaign and her claims that she had been duped by her husband–campaign manager.

Yet no member, perhaps ever, could match the level of press interest in the GOP Speaker of the House, Newt Gingrich. Although a good deal of his coverage pertained to allegations of ethics breaches, to be sure, almost everything that he did attracted attention. He was *Time* magazine's no-surprise choice for Man of the Year in 1995. The nature of his coverage ultimately became a liability to the GOP, and by year's end, Gingrich tried to adopt a lower public profile.

Covering the Speaker

It would be impossible to completely chronicle Gingrich's elite press coverage since his rise to the speakership. There was simply too much of it. As Meg Greenfield put it, Gingrich was the "Dominator-in-Chief of the news."[147] Many journalists speculated about Gingrich running for president.[148] Some stories treated the new Speaker as though he were on a par in importance with the president.[149] A *Wall Street Journal* profile likened Gingrich's effect on the nation to a strong cup of coffee. "He has made the nation sit up and take notice of the government, but he is leaving people jittery."[150] Jack E. White underscored that some found Gingrich's rise to prominence frightening: "Let's face it: To most African Americans Newt Gingrich is one scary white man."[151]

Each of the major publications examined here ran extensive profiles of the Speaker chronicling his past and rise to national power. For example, the *Washington Post* alone featured a four-part front-page series entitled "Mr. Speaker: The Rise of Newt Gingrich." Each of the articles appeared above the fold on page one and continued for two full additional pages of text and pictures. There was enough material in these articles alone to fill a book.[152] The *Post*'s "Inside the Revolution" series also featured a lengthy front-page piece on how Gingrich held the GOP coalition together in the House during a period of pressure to back down from some of its agenda.[153] The *Post* also published a lengthy front-page story based on a two-hour Gingrich luncheon with the newspaper's reporters and editors.[154] As did the *Post*, other sources included many unflattering stories about Gingrich's legislative record and personal life in their lengthy profiles.[155]

There is a certain irony to the fact that Gingrich so effectively used the media for years to plot his rise to national prominence, and yet once he achieved that goal, his coverage was relentlessly negative. He both used the media to promote himself and his goals and lambasted those who covered him as liberal "elitists" and even "socialists."[156] As Jonathan Alter wrote, "The press has certainly done its part to keep the poison flowing in the other direction." Alter chose as especially noteworthy the hypernegative coverage of Gingrich in the *New York Times*, which featured such commentaries about the Speaker as "The Politics of Meanness," "A Simple Case of Fraud," and "Newt Gingrich, Authoritarian."[157] A post–1994 elections *National Journal* article entitled "Is the 'Elite' Press Out to Get Newt?" concluded that the Speaker indeed already had been the victim of intensely negative coverage.[158] The Center for Media and Public Affairs found that 69 percent of

Gingrich's elite press coverage during the first one hundred days of the session was negative.[159]

Gingrich fancied himself as a kind of philosopher-leader. He therefore openly engaged in speculation about policy alternatives that led to criticism of many of his outlandish-seeming ideas. For example, he suggested on "Meet the Press" that states be allowed to place nonorphaned children in orphanages as an alternative to government support. He speculated that cutbacks in social programs would invigorate charitable giving to the poor. Both comments invited strong criticism.[160]

To be sure, a good deal of the negative coverage could be attributed to the Speaker's penchant for making controversial and sometimes distasteful statements. For example, at one point he referred to Democrats as "the enemy of normal Americans"—a comment that brought understandably outraged editorial rebuke.[161] He once called the House Democratic party leadership the "cocaine-selling, check-bouncing, big-spending, left-wing petty dictatorship." He claimed that LBJ was responsible for more deaths from his Great Society programs than from his policies in Vietnam. When national media attention focused on the tragedy of a mother drowning her two children, Gingrich blamed the event on Democratic party philosophy. Even after enormous criticism for that comment, he later blamed a horrible murder in which an infant was torn from the murdered woman's womb on the Democratic-created welfare state. At one point, Gingrich referred to the president and Mrs. Clinton as "counterculture McGoverniks" and then alleged, without fact, that some White House staffers were recreational drug users. A widely reported Gingrich comment came from a college-class lecture in which he stated that women were not suited to combat because "females have biological problems staying in a ditch for thirty days because they get infections."[162] Harsh press criticism for such comments was fair, although the Speaker's defenders believed that media interest in controversial statements too often overwhelmed the man's more serious ideas.

But a good deal of the press criticism also reeked of tabloidlike cynicism. The most conspicuous example was the overwhelmingly harsh response to the Speaker accepting a large advance from a publisher to write two books. There was nothing illegal about the contract, as a House Ethics Committee report later concluded. Yet because the owner of the publishing company had a direct interest in legislation before Congress, many assumed that Gingrich had entered into an unseemly deal. Charges of unethical conduct surrounded Gingrich's press coverage during his first year as Speaker.[163] Even those who felt that the critics had gone too far in questioning Gingrich's ethics found a way to turn the issue against him. For example, Richard Cohen attributed the controversy over the book deal to the kind of "ethical frenzy" that too often takes over the Washington community at the slightest hint of possible wrongdoing. Yet, Cohen pointed out, it was Gingrich who had earlier contributed to and benefited politically from the rise of ethical frenzies (for example, by his attacks on the former Democratic Speaker Jim Wright).[164] William Raspberry agreed that Gingrich was merely suffering the fate that he had inflicted on others: "The acerbic tongue, general nastiness and overweening self-righteousness that Gingrich rode to his new job as speaker of the House make it almost poetic that he's now getting what he so diffidently gave."[165]

Gingrich relinquished his book advance, although he did not forgo any royalties. His troubles did not stop there. News reports maintained that Gingrich used his position of influence to aid his political benefactors.[166] Journalists picked through his many often controversial statements and writings to find and report any misstatements or contradictions.[167] They also uncovered some controversial opinions of his choice for House historian, resulting in a barrage of criticism for selecting her.

The Speaker did the most damage to his own repute when he admitted that his hard-line response in budget negotiations with the White House had been influenced, in part, by what he perceived as discourteous treatment by the president. In brief, Gingrich alleged that during a twenty-five-hour flight on Air Force One to Israel to attend the funeral of the prime minister, Clinton had relegated the Speaker to the back of the plane. Editorial cartoonists and headline writers had great fun mocking this admission that Gingrich had partially caused a government shutdown because he did not get to sit in the front of the plane. The *New York Daily News*, in its most memorable tabloid cover since "Ford to City: Drop Dead," depicted Gingrich as a child in diapers with the screaming bold headline "CRY BABY."[168] All of the sources studied here featured either pictures or descriptions of the *Daily News* cover. *Newsweek* published a comic of Gingrich in diapers sitting next to Bob Dole in an airplane, crying "I wanna sit up front. . . . Waaaa!"[169] Mary McGrory asked, "Did Gingrich have to shut down the government over it?"[170] *Time* said that Gingrich's behavior helped Dole's presidential campaign "by fueling the impression that it might be time to put an adult in charge to end the gridlock."[171] The press and the public largely blamed Gingrich and the GOP in Congress for the budget stalemates in 1995.

Gingrich's coverage had by the end of the year become so relentlessly negative that he announced a plan to lower his public profile. The result: lengthy front-page stories followed the announcement.[172] At the end of 1994, in its year-in-perspective issue, *Newsweek* featured a Dickensian cartoon of Gingrich on the cover as "The Gingrich Who Stole Christmas." The end-of-1995 issue said that Gingrich had gone from the "man of the year" to "just another blowhard." *Time* featured him on the cover as its 1995 "Man of the Year." The cover photo, to put it mildly, was unflattering, even ominous looking. *Time* columnist Margaret Carlson explained that being on the cover as the magazine's "Man of the Year" was not intended as a compliment: "Remember . . . Hitler was on the cover twice. Stalin was on the cover."[173] *Time*'s report proclaimed the Speaker "the greatest liability to the revolution he launched."[174] A *U.S. News* item agreed that "with that big mouth, he hurts his own revolution."[175] The magazine's review of Gingrich's first year as Speaker offered the following: "He has, to some extent, already been Quayle-ized—frozen in a frame in the public's mind. If Quayle was dumb, Gingrich is mean. Gingrich, a master of political caricature, has now become one." The article acknowledged nonetheless that Gingrich was a skillful legislative leader.[176] By the end of 1995, the *Time*/CNN poll revealed, only 24 percent of the public had a favorable view of Gingrich, and only 9 percent said that they would like to see him as president. A majority said that he had failed to bring "needed change to government."[177]

CONCLUSION

Recent congressional coverage remains as abysmal as in the late 1980s and early 1990s. Despite Congress's attempts at fundamental change, the public clamors for greater legislative efficiency, an end to partisan squabbling, lower tax burdens, and continued government support for popular programs. Opinion polls since the late 1980s consistently show that public disapproval of Congress outpaces favorable opinion by about a 2–1 margin. It seems that no matter what Congress does, people complain. Neither partisan nor policy change has improved the coverage of Congress and public views of its activities. The extensive coverage of Speaker Gingrich evidenced once again the press preference for stories about colorful personalities and controversy rather than process and policy.

NOTES

1. *Newsweek* cover, January 8, 1996.

2. David E. Rosenbaum, "Public Calls Lawmakers Corrupt and Pampered," *New York Times*, October 10, 1991, p. B17.

3. Richard Morin and Helen Dewar, "Approval of Congress Hits All-Time Low, Poll Finds," *Washington Post*, March 20, 1992, p. A16.

4. David Broder, "Yes, There Are Good People in Congress," *Washington Post*, November 6, 1991, p. A25. Another columnist, Michael Kinsley, decried the "hypocrisy" of those leading the criticism of Congress, the "columnists and commentators who make many times what a member of Congress does, and who are far more steeped in the culture of Washington than a congressman who goes home every weekend." See Michael Kinsley, "Hypocrisy from the Heartland," *Washington Post*, October 12, 1991, p. A25.

5. "Sham and Shame," *Wall Street Journal*, March 4, 1991, p. A8.

6. "Constituent Disservice," *Wall Street Journal*, April 18, 1991, p. A16.

7. "Kitegate Spills Over," *Wall Street Journal*, October 4, 1991, p. A14.

8. "Congress's Non-Bank Bank," *Wall Street Journal*, September 25, 1991, p. A10. See also "A New Political Ballgame," *Wall Street Journal*, October 16, 1991, p. A16.

9. "Eating Ethics," *New York Times*, October 8, 1991, p. A24.

10. "House Cleaning: Also Senate," *New York Times*, October 20, 1991, sec. 4, p. 14.

11. "The Bouncing Bank Cleanup Lags," *New York Times*, October 2, 1991, p. A22.

12. "Eating Ethics," p. A24.

13. "Come Clean on the House Bank," *New York Times*, March 11, 1992, p. A22.

14. "Not All Bounces Are Bad," *New York Times*, March 19, 1992, p. A22.

15. "Listen to the Anger," *New York Times*, March 26, 1992, p. A22.

16. "Worse Than the House Bank," *New York Times*, March 14, 1992, p. 24.

17. "El Al D'Amato," *New York Times*, December 4, 1991, p. A26.

18. "The Keating None?" *New York Times*, October 23, 1991, p. A22.

19. "The Keating One Hundred," *New York Times*, November 21, 1991, p. A26.

20. "Bounce the House Bank," *Washington Post*, September 23, 1991, p. A10. See also "The Speaker Has Spoken—And Well," *Washington Post*, September 29, 1991, p. C6; "The House Names Names," *Washington Post*, April 19, 1992, p. C6; "The House Bank (Cont'd)," *Washington Post*, April 28, 1992, p. A14.

21. Jill Abramson and David Rogers, "The Keating 535," *Wall Street Journal*, January 10, 1991, p. A1.

22. Nancy Gibbs, "Perk City," *Time*, October 14, 1991, p. 18.

23. Ibid., 19–20.

24. Ibid., p. 20.

25. Margaret Carlson, "The Ultimate Men's Club," *Time*, October 21, 1991, p. 50.

26. Ibid., pp. 50–51. See also Eleanor Clift, "Congress: The Ultimate Men's Club," *Newsweek*, October 21, 1991, p. 32.

27. Larry Martz and Eleanor Clift, "Who Says There's No Free Lunch?" *Newsweek*, October 14, 1991, p. 30.

28. Gloria Borger, "Blowing the Lid on Kiters Inc.," *U.S. News and World Report*, March 23, 1992, p. 36.

29. Gloria Borger, Stephen J. Hedges, and Gary Cohen, "Congress: Life among the Ruins," *U.S. News and World Report*, March 30, 1992, pp. 24–25.

30. Tom Kenworthy, "Is the House Haunted by Midnight?" *Washington Post*, March 14, 1992, p. A4.

31. Guy Gugliotta and Kenneth J. Cooper, "String of House Scandals Saps Public Confidence," *Washington Post*, March 11, 1992, pp. A1, A6. See also Howard Kurtz, "Hill Perks: Old Story Resonates Anew," *Washington Post*, April 9, 1992, p. A4. Other news stories focused on such different problems troubling Congress as the dominance of symbolism over substance, fragmentation, lack of deference to leadership, and divided government. See Adam Clymer, "An Institution under Duress," *New York Times*, November 10, 1991, p. A23; Adam Clymer, "Tarnished Congress," *New York Times*, November 29, 1991, p. D7; Helen Dewar, "On Capitol Hill, Symbols Triumph," *Washington Post*, November 26, 1991, pp. A1, A4.

32. David Gergen, "Profiles in Privilege," *U.S. News and World Report*, October 14, 1991, p. 104.

33. George F. Will, "Perpetual Incumbency Machine," *Washington Post*, November 10, 1991, p. C7.

34. George F. Will, "Term Limits: Antitrust in Politics," *Washington Post*, November 3, 1991, p. C7. See also his other columns on this topic: "A Case for Term Limits," *Newsweek*, October 21, 1991, p. 76; "No More Careerists in Congress," *Washington Post*, October 1, 1992, p. A27; "What Voters Did for the System," *Washington Post*, November 12, 1992, p. A21.

35. Rowland Evans and Robert Novak, "No Bashing of Brethren," *Washington Post*, October 2, 1991, p. A23.

36. Michael Kramer, "Shame on Them All," *Time*, October 21, 1991, p. 46.

37. Ibid., p. 47.

38. Stanley Cloud, "Bums of the Year," *Time*, January 6, 1992, p. 48. This column was accompanied by three drawings: one of a pig speaking into a group of microphones, one of the Capitol dome coming apart, and one of several hands dipping into a large pile of cash.

39. Tom Kenworthy, "Keep the Bums In!" *Washington Post*, April 26, 1992, p. C5.

40. Haynes Johnson, "A Bankruptcy of Principles," *Washington Post*, October 4, 1991, p. A2.

41. Mary McGrory, "Toxic Spring in Washington," *Washington Post*, April 5, 1992, p. C5.

42. William Safire, "Hail to the House," *New York Times*, October 7, 1991, p. A17.

43. Paul Gigot, "The Voters Flex before Throwing the Bums Out," *Wall Street Journal*, March 6, 1992, p. A8.

44. Meg Greenfield, "Everyone vs. Congress," *Washington Post*, November 5, 1991, p. A21. See also Meg Greenfield, "The Judges on the Hill," *Washington Post*, October 8, 1991, p. A19.

45. David S. Broder, "House at Play," *Washington Post*, March 17, 1992, p. A17. A drawing of a rubber check bouncing over the Capitol accompanied the Broder column. See also David Broder, "The Democrats' Debit," *Washington Post*, September 25, 1991, p. A25.

46. Helen Dewar, "102d Congress Often Was Thwarted by Senate Filibusters and Bush Vetoes," *Washington Post*, October 11, 1992, p. A33. See also Helen Dewar, " 'Much Needs to be Done' in Final Days of 102d Congress," August 14, 1992, p. A8.

47. Gloria Borger, "A Capitol Idea: Goodnight to All That," *U.S. News and World Report*, October 19, 1992, p. 8.

48. Cited in "Low-Grade Government," *USA Today*, September 3, 1992, p. A1.

49. See Adam Clymer, "Public Believes Worst on Bank Scandal," *New York Times*, April 2, 1992, p. D21.

50. Political humorists took advantage of the negative coverage of Congress to lampoon the institution. See Tony Kornheiser, "The System of Checks and Bounces," *Washington Post*, October 6, 1991, p. F1. One opinion column, by a political scientist, described the charges against Congress in the press as "wildly distorted, patently unfair and hypocritical." See Norman Ornstein, "Congress Confidential," *Washington Post*, November 3, 1991, p. C5. I found no other article that seriously sought to set the record straight on the various charges against Congress.

51. Adam Clymer, "Congress Hunts for Way to Gain a Little Respect," *New York Times*, July 23, 1992, p. A20.

52. Kevin Merida, "Polishing Congress's Tarnished Image," *Washington Post*, January 25, 1994, pp. A1, A4.

53. Kevin Merida, "America's Latest Soap: As Congress Turns," *Washington Post*, June 5, 1994, pp. A1, A19.

54. "Congress's Image Problem," *Washington Post*, June 5, 1994, p. C6.

55. "To Know Congress . . . , " *Wall Street Journal*, July 7, 1994, p. A12.

56. "Mood of the Country," *Wall Street Journal*, September 9, 1994, p. A14.

57. "The Pork Barrel Barons," *U.S. News and World Report*, February 21, 1994, cover.

58. "The Senate's Most Precious Turf," *Washington Post*, April 25, 1994, p. A16. The Senate attracted widespread editorial scorn for trying to disguise the parking perk by changing the sign at National Airport from "RESERVED PARKING/SUPREME COURT JUSTICES/MEMBERS OF CONGRESS/DIPLOMATIC CORPS" to "RESTRICTED PARKING/AUTHORIZED USERS ONLY."

59. George F. Will, "Why Washington Grieves (2)," *Washington Post*, June 2, 1994, p. A23. See also David S. Broder, "Why Washington Grieves (1)," and Richard Cohen " 'Stand Fast Rosty,' They Told Him," *Washington Post*, June 2,

1944, p. A23; Bob Cohn, "Rostenkowski's Choice," *Newsweek*, May 30, 1994, p. 49.

60. See Dan Balz and Eric Pianin, "Another Bruise for a Beleaguered Institution," *Washington Post*, June 1, 1994, pp. A1, A16.

61. Kenneth J. Cooper and Kevin Merida, "Lawmakers Reveal That Travel Is Still Frequent Gift of Lobbyists," *Washington Post*, June 11, 1994, p. A12; Helen Dewar and Eric Pianin, "Senators Heed Constituents on Lifestyle," *Washington Post*, June 15, 1994, p. A8; Liz Spayd, "Local Lawmakers Also Board House's Travel Gravy Train," *Washington Post*, June 11, 1994, p. A12.

62. "Send Them Home?" *Washington Post*, August 24, 1994, p. A18.

63. "The Hollow Branch," *Washington Post*, August 26, 1994, p. A24; "Perhaps the Worst Congress," *Washington Post*, October 7, 1994, p. A24; "Abuse of Sausage Making," *Washington Post*, August 26, 1994, p. A24. See also "Blame Game," *Washington Post*, October 3, 1994, p. A18; "Congress and the Clock," *Washington Post*, July 5, 1994, p. A14; Helen Dewar and Kenneth J. Cooper, "103d Congress Started Fast But Collapsed at Finish Line," *Washington Post*, October 9, 1994, pp. A1, A21. Congressional scholars, by contrast, for the most part rated the 103d Congress as productive. See Stephen Gettinger, "View from the Ivory Tower More Rosy Than Media's," *Congressional Quarterly Weekly Report*, October 8, 1994, p. 2850.

64. "Capitol Hill Follies: How TV Has Covered the 103d Congress," *Media Monitor*, September/October 1994, p. 3.

65. Richard L. Berke, "For Voters, Hope Gives Way to Anger, Fear, and Cynicism," *New York Times*, October 10, 1994, pp. A1, A14.

66. Representative Barney Frank (D–Mass.) quoted in Richard Harwood, "The Voters' IQ," *Washington Post*, October 24, 1994, p. A19.

67. "Gridlock's Political Price," *New York Times*, October 9, 1994, sec. 4, p. 14. See also Michael Barone, "The Last Democratic House?" *U.S. News and World Report*, July 18, 1994, p. 30.

68. David S. Broder, "Democrats Run a Risk in Running against '80s," *Washington Post*, October 12, 1994, pp. A1, A8.

69. Robin Toner, "Image of Capitol Maligned by Outsiders, and Insiders," *New York Times*, October 16, 1994, pp. 1, 24. See also Karen Tumulty, "The Price of Pork," *Time*, November 7, 1994, pp. 37–39.

70. Quoted in Gerald F. Seib, "Campaign Memo: It's Government, Stupid, in 1994," *Wall Street Journal*, October 19, 1994, p. A22.

71. Ibid.

72. John H. Fund, "The Revolution of 1994," *Wall Street Journal*, October 19, 1994, p. A20.

73. Richard Lacayo, "Bringing Down the House," *Time*, November 7, 1994, pp. 28–36.

74. A study of major television network news coverage of Gingrich during the campaign showed that negative stories outpaced positive ones by a 4–1 ratio. "The

November Surprise: TV News Coverage of the 1994 Elections," *Media Monitor*, November/December 1994, p. 5.

75. John F. Stacks, "Stampede!" *Time*, November 21, 1994, p. 48.

76. "Mr. Clinton's Future and the G.O.P.," *New York Times*, December 6, 1994, p. 22; "Mr. Gingrich's Leaner House," *New York Times*, December 8, 1994, p. 34.

77. See, for example, E. J. Dionne, Jr., "A Shift, Not a Mandate," *Washington Post*, November 22, 1994, p. A21; William Raspberry, "It Doesn't Work," *Washington Post*, November 23, 1994, p. A19.

78. Dan Goodgame, "Right Makes Might," *Time*, November 21, 1994, p. 61.

79. Stacks, "Stampede!" p. 48.

80. Goodgame, "Right Makes Might," p. 54.

81. Richard L. Berke, "Asked to Place Blame, Americans in Surveys Chose: All of the Above," *New York Times*, November 10, 1994, p. B1.

82. Gerald F. Seib, "Voters, Having Changed Congress, Now Want Congress to Change Washington, Poll Indicates," *Wall Street Journal*, November 11, 1994, p. A16.

83. Evan Thomas, "A Guide to the First 100 Days," *Newsweek*, January 9, 1995, p. 22.

84. Gloria Borger, "Welcome to Gingrich Nation," *U.S. News and World Report*, November 21, 1994, p. 44.

85. "The Sea Change," *Washington Post*, November 10, 1994, p. A24.

86. "Mr. Clinton's Missive," *Washington Post*, January 9, 1995, p. A16.

87. "Dr. Fell's Election," *New York Times*, November 10, 1994, p. A34.

88. Joe Klein, "The New, New Deal," *Newsweek*, December 26, 1994/January 2, 1995, p. 19.

89. Steven Waldman, "Creating a Congressional Counterculture," *Newsweek*, January 16, 1995, p. 18.

90. Steven V. Roberts, "Sea Change," *U.S. News and World Report*, November 21, 1994, p. 40.

91. George F. Will, "Reagan's Third Victory," *Washington Post*, November 10, 1994, p. A25. Other conservatives included Jeane Kirkpatrick, Thomas Sowell, and William Kristol, all cited in Max Frankel, "Pick a Mandate," *New York Times Magazine*, December 4, 1994, p. 56.

92. Richard Morin and Barbara Vobejda, " '94 May Be the Year of the Man," *Washington Post*, November 10, 1994, p. A27.

93. Raspberry's, Leo's, and Klein's commentaries are cited in Frankel, "Pick a Mandate," p. 56.

94. Richard Lacayo, "After the Revolution," *Time*, November 28, 1994, p. 31; David E. Rosenbaum, "Strong Speaker, Strong House? One Doesn't Necessarily Follow the Other," *New York Times*, December 4, 1994, p. 32.

95. Howard Fineman, "Revenge of the Right," *Newsweek*, November 21, 1994, p. 38.

96. Borger, "Welcome to Gingrich Nation," p. 44.

97. "Losing in Style," *U.S. News and World Report*, December 12, 1994, p. 34.

98. Mortimer B. Zuckerman, "Behind the Voters' Message," *U.S. News and World Report*, November 21, 1994, p. 100.

99. Robert J. Samuelson, "The Public Trust: Handle with Care," *Washington Post*, January 4, 1995, p. A15.

100. Evan Thomas, "Goodbye Welfare State," *Newsweek*, November 21, 1994, p. 44.

101. See Tom Kenworthy, "GOP Plan to Broaden Property Rights Could Cost Public Dearly," *Washington Post*, December 13, 1994, p. A7; "Not a Green Congress," *Washington Post*, November 22, 1994, p. A20.

102. Thomas, "Guide to the First 100 Days," p. 24.

103. Thomas, "Goodbye Welfare State," p. 44.

104. Richard Lacayo, "Taming the Troops," *Time*, February 6, 1995, pp. 22, 24.

105. Steven V. Roberts, "Squaring Off over Values," *U.S. News and World Report*, November 28, 1994, pp. 48–49.

106. Roberts, "Sea Change," p. 40.

107. "A New Deal," *Wall Street Journal*, January 4, 1995, p. A12. See also Meg Greenfield, "Prescription Politics," *Washington Post*, January 9, 1995, p. A17.

108. "The Contract So Far," *Washington Post*, March 6, 1995, p. A16.

109. David S. Broder, "The Right Time for a Test of Ideas," *Washington Post*, February 1, 1995, p. A19.

110. David S. Broder, "Freshmen Orientation," *Washington Post*, January 4, 1995, p. A15.

111. "Welcome to the 104th," *Washington Post*, January 4, 1995, p. A14.

112. "Mr. Clinton's Missive," p. A16.

113. Robert D. Novak, "Retiring on Pensions," *Washington Post*, January 2, 1995, p. A19. After the first hundred days, the *Wall Street Journal* ("Washington Wire," April 7, 1995, p. A1) complained that despite the GOP pledge to sell a House office building in the first hundred days, no "for sale" signs had yet appeared.

114. Edward Walsh, "GOP Confronts a Wary Public," *Washington Post*, January 8, 1995, pp. A1, A8.

115. Helen Dewar, "In Tradition-bound Senate, the Revolution Must Wait," *Washington Post*, January 6, 1995, pp. A1, A5.

116. See, for example, Jack Anderson and Michael Binstein, "Spare Change for a New Perk," *Washington Post*, January 22, 1995, p. C7.

117. See Jill Abramson and Timothy Noah, "In GOP-controlled Congress, Lobbyists Remain as Powerful As Ever—And Perhaps More Visible," *Wall Street Journal*, April 20, 1995, p. A14; Thomas Rosenstiel, "The 'Shiites' of the House," *Newsweek*, February 6, 1995, pp. 18–19.

118. Waldman, "Creating a Congressional Counterculture," p. 19.

119. Guy Gugliotta, "At Manufacturers' Seminar on Hill, There's Room for Improvement," *Washington Post*, February 2, 1995, p. A8.

120. Robert D. Novak, "Term Limit Turnaround," *Washington Post*, March 9, 1995, p. A21.

121. "The Term-Limits Scam," *Washington Post*, March 12, 1995, p. C6. See also "Term Limits, R.I.P.," *Washington Post*, April 12, 1995, p. A24; "We Already Have Term Limits," *Washington Post*, March 29, 1995, p. A22; David S. Broder, "Term Limits: The Good Fight," *Washington Post*, April 5, 1995, p. A19; William Claiborne, "Anger at Term Limits Defeat Echoes Loudly across Nation," *Washington Post*, March 31, 1995, pp. A1, A24; Guy Gugliotta, "Young, Old Cast Slurs As GOP Unity Cracks," *Washington Post*, March 30, 1995, pp. A1, A7; George F. Will, "No Heavy Lifting, Please," *Washington Post*, February 9, 1995, p. A29; George F. Will, "Term Limits: This Battle Will Go On," *Washington Post*, May 24, 1995, p. A25.

122. One example was Majority Leader Richard Armey's (R–Texas) slur of homosexual congressman Barney Frank (D–Mass.) as "Barney Fag." *Newsweek* pointed out that news coverage of that comment outpaced Senate passage of a crucial unfunded-mandates bill on the same day. Rosenstiel, " 'Shiites' of the House," pp. 18–19.

123. Mary McGrory, "Hatfield's Capitol Punishment," *Washington Post*, March 9, 1995, p. A2.

124. Charles Krauthammer, "The Watershed Election of 1996," *Washington Post*, March 31, 1995, p. A31.

125. See Tom Kenworthy, "Truth Is Victim in Rules Debate," *Washington Post*, March 19, 1995, pp. A1, A12.

126. Thomas Rosenstiel, "Why Newt Is No Joke," *Newsweek*, April 10, 1995, p. 26.

127. Robert J. Samuelson, "Deliver Now, Pay Later," *Washington Post*, April 12, 1995, p. A25.

128. David S. Broder, "Shift to the Senate," *Washington Post*, April 12, 1995, p. A25. See also "The New Congress . . . So Far," *Washington Post*, April 9, 1995, p. C6.

129. "Media Won't Sign On to G.O.P. Contract," *Political Newswatch* (Center for Media and Public Affairs), April 20, 1995, p. 7.

130. "The New Congress . . . So Far," p. C6; see also David S. Broder, "When Republicans Monopolize the Debate," *Washington Post*, December 14, 1994, p A25; Kenneth J. Cooper and Helen Dewar, "100 Days Down but Senate to Go for Most 'Contract' Items," *Washington Post*, April 9, 1995, pp. A6, A7; Paul A. Gigot, "Altered States: The Contract's Real Victory," *Wall Street Journal*, April 7, 1995, p. A14; James Popkin, "They Think They Can," *U.S. News and World Report*, April 10, 1995, pp. 26–32; David Rogers and Gerald F. Seib, "GOP, Despite Slips, Manages to Change Government's Course," *Wall Street Journal*, April 7, 1995, pp. A1, A6; Samuelson, "Deliver Now, Pay Later," p. A25.

131. Bruce B. Auster, "Help Yourself to Some Pork," *U.S. News and World Report*, July 24, 1995, p. 34; Rich Thomas, "Pork Goes Republican," *Newsweek*, August 14, 1995, p. 34.

132. Abramson and Noah, "In GOP-controlled Congress, Lobbyists Remain As Powerful As Ever—and Perhaps More Visible," p. A14; see also Jeffrey H. Birnbaum, "The Thursday Regulars," *Time*, March 27, 1995, pp. 30–31.

133. "Would-Be Reformers," *Washington Post*, May 4, 1995, p. A20. See also David Bowermaster, "Dancing to an Old Tune," *U.S. News and World Report*, July 17, 1995, pp. 20–22.

134. Richard L. Berke, "One Change Is Not in the Contract," *New York Times*, April 9, 1995, sec. 4, p. 3.

135. David Maraniss and Michael Weisskopf, "Speaker and His Directors Make the Cash Flow Right," *Washington Post*, November 27, 1995, p. A1.

136. Bruce B. Auster, "Tantrums, Taxes, & Tactics," *U.S. News and World Report*, November 27, 1995, pp. 34–39; Gloria Borger, "Will It Be History or Hysteria?" *U.S. News and World Report*, December 4, 1995, p. 61; Jill Smolowe, "Sticks and Stones," *Time*, November 27, 1995, pp. 52–56; Rich Thomas and Steven Waldman, "What the Fight's About," *Newsweek*, December 4, 1995, pp. 36–37; Bill Turque and Evan Thomas, "Missing the Moment," *Newsweek*, November 27, 1995, pp. 26–29.

137. "Showdown!" *U.S. News and World Report*, November 27, 1995 (cover).

138. Colbert I. King, "When 'Bureaucrats' Become Real People," *Washington Post*, December 30, 1995, p. A19.

139. See, for example, Richard Morin, "Public Sides with Clinton in Fiscal Fight," *Washington Post*, November 21, 1995, p. A4.

140. See "Chairman Kasich's Budget . . . , " *Washington Post*, May 12, 1995, p. A24.

141. E. J. Dionne, Jr., "The Democrats' Turn," *Washington Post*, May 16, 1995, p. A17; Steven Pearlstein, " 'Hope' Is a Number in GOP Math," *Washington Post*, May 17, 1995, pp. A1, A6.

142. Jim Hoagland, "Fiscally Feckless," *Washington Post*, April 9, 1995, p. C7.

143. "A Bad Bill in the House," *Washington Post*, March 22, 1995, p. A20.

144. Russell Baker, "Time for the Pain," *New York Times*, May 13, 1995, p. A19; David Gergen, "The GOP's 'Fairness Doctrine?' " *U.S. News and World Report*, November 13, 1995, p. 123; Mary McGrory, "Armey of the Shameless," *Washington Post*, July 16, 1995, pp. C1, C2; "Will Charity Fill the Gap?" *Washington Post*, July 11, 1995, p. A16.

145. See, for example, Gloria Borger, "Capitol Hill's Two-Ring Circus," *U.S. News and World Report*, July 31, 1995, p. 30; Mary McGrory, "Dog Days for the News," *Washington Post*, July 18, 1995, p. A2; Mary McGrory, "Whitewater-Waco Weariness," *Washington Post*, July 20, 1995, p. A2. Even congressional actions that some deemed praiseworthy were attended with sarcastic headlines.

See, for example, Michael Barone, "Attention: Congress Acting Sensibly," *U.S. News and World Report*, March 20, 1995, p. 44.

146. Helen Dewar, "Historic Session Leaves Minor Legislative Legacy," *Washington Post*, January 2, 1996, p. A1.

147. Meg Greenfield, "Misplaying Gingrich," *Washington Post*, December 12, 1994, p. A23.

148. Howard Fineman, "President Newt?" *Newsweek*, June 19, 1995, pp. 34–36; Joe Klein, "Will Newt Run for President?" *Newsweek*, May 8, 1995, p. 47; "Newt Gingrich for President?" *Newsweek*, January 23, 1995, p. 23.

149. See, for example, James Carney and Karen Tumulty, "Master of the House," *Time*, January 16, 1995, pp. 24–31.

150. David Rogers and Phil Kuntz, "Jump-Start: How Gingrich Grabbed Power and Attention," *Wall Street Journal*, January 19, 1995, pp. A1, A12.

151. Jack E. White, "Deal with the Devil," *Time*, January 16, 1995, p. 29.

152. Dale Russakoff, "He Knew What He Wanted," *Washington Post*, December 18, 1994, pp. A1, A28, A29; Dale Russakoff and Dan Balz, "After Political Victory, a Personal Revolution," *Washington Post*, December 19, 1994, pp. A1, A18, A19; Dan Balz and Charles R. Babcock, "Gingrich Allies Made Waves and Impression," *Washington Post*, December 20, 1994, pp. A1, A14, A15; Dan Balz and Serge F. Kovaleski, "Gingrich Divided GOP, Conquered the Agenda," *Washington Post*, December 21, 1994, pp. A1, A18, A19.

153. Michael Weisskopf and David Maraniss, "In a Moment of Crisis, the Speaker Persuades," *Washington Post*, August 13, 1995, pp. A1, A8.

154. Kenneth J. Cooper, "Gingrich Pledges Major Package of Spending Cuts Early Next Year," *Washington Post*, December 13, 1994, pp. A1, A6. After having contributed heavily to the Gingrich profile, the newspaper followed up with a lengthy front-page analysis of how he was handling the enormous scrutiny and attention. See Kenneth J. Cooper, "Speaker Tries to Adjust to Life in the Spotlight," *Washington Post*, January 11, 1995, pp. A1, A6.

155. See, for example, Howard Fineman, "The Warrior," *Newsweek*, January 9, 1995, pp. 28–34.

156. See Howard Kurtz, "Gingrich Criticizes 'Nit-Picking' Media," *Washington Post*, January 10, 1995, p. A7; Howard Kurtz and Ann Devroy, "Speaker Rails against Media 'Socialists,' " *Washington Post*, March 8, 1995, p. A4.

157. Jonathan Alter, "Spiro Agnew with Brains," *Newsweek*, November 28, 1994, p. 34.

158. Paul Starobin, "Is the 'Elite' Press Out to Get Newt?" *National Journal*, November 26, 1994, pp. 2788ff.

159. "Media Won't Sign On to G.O.P. Contract," p. 9.

160. See, for example, Richard Cohen, "Orphanages: Giving Gingrich the Dickens," *Washington Post*, December 6, 1994, p. A19; Ellen Goodman, "Back to Orphanages," *Washington Post*, November 19, 1994, p. A17.

161. For example, the *Post* retorted, "Where does a politician who wants to exercise substantial power get off deciding who is and who isn't a 'normal' American?" ("Mr. Gingrich and What's 'Normal,' " *Washington Post*, October 17, 1994, p. A18).

162. Quoted in *Newsweek*, December 25, 1995/January 1, 1996, p. 49.

163. See, for example, the *Newsweek* cover story "And Now, Newtgate," December 18, 1995, and the *U.S. News and World Report* cover "Gingrich on the Hot Seat," December 18, 1995; also, Howard Fineman, "Gingrich Goes Ballistic," *Newsweek*, January 30, 1995, pp. 32–32b; Mark Hosenball and Michael Isikoff, "Why Newt's in Trouble," *Newsweek*, December 18, 1995, pp. 36–37; Weston Kosova and Michael Isikoff, "The Trouble with Newt," *Newsweek*, December 11, 1995, p. 40; Richard Lacayo, "Newt's Cash Machine," *Time*, December 18, 1995, pp. 39–40; "The Speaker and the Book," *Washington Post*, January 22, 1995, p. C6; "The Gingrich Case," *Washington Post*, December 8, 1995, p. A26; "Gingrich Inc.," *Washington Post*, April 2, 1995, p. C6.

164. Richard Cohen, "Bum Rap on Gingrich," *Washington Post*, January 3, 1995, p. A15.

165. William Raspberry, "Uglier Than Gridlock," *Washington Post*, January 25, 1995, p. A25.

166. Serge F. Kovaleski and R. H. Melton, "Gingrich Sings Praises of Many Benefactors," *Washington Post*, March 20, 1995, pp. A1, A8.

167. Richard Cohen, "Gingrich, Talking Up a Storm," *Washington Post*, March 9, 1995, p. A21; Richard Cohen, "The Speaker as Scribe," *Washington Post*, July 6, 1995, p. A21; Kenneth J. Cooper, "Gingrich Acknowledges a Few Academic Errors," *Washington Post*, March 8, 1995, p. A4; R. H. Melton, "Booked-up Speaker Tests Market," *Washington Post*, July 7, 1995, p. A4.

168. *New York Daily News*, November 16, 1995.

169. *Newsweek*, November 27, 1995, p. 25.

170. Mary McGrory, "Cage aux Fools," *Washington Post*, November 19, 1995, pp. C1, C6. See also Mary McGrory, "Newt-Mare Come True," *Washington Post*, December 10, 1995, pp. C1, C5.

171. Jill Smolowe, "Sticks and Stones," *Time*, November 27, 1995, pp. 52–56.

172. Dan Balz and John E. Yang, "Gingrich to Lower His Public Profile," *Washington Post*, December 2, 1995, pp. A1, A8.

173. Quoted in Howard Kurtz, "A Time-worn Newt Gingrich," *Washington Post*, December 19, 1995, pp. B1, B2.

174. Nancy Gibbs and Karen Tumulty, "Master of the House," *Time*, December 25, 1995/January 1, 1996, p. 54.

175. "Pulse Points," *U.S. News and World Report*, January 8, 1996, p. 17.

176. Gloria Borger, "Rebel without a Pause," *U.S. News and World Report*, January 8, 1996, p. 25.

177. Ibid., p. 60.

Chapter Six

Contempt of Congress:
Sources and Recommendations

Since World War II, the press has generally held Congress in low esteem. Deliberative, unexciting, usually uneventful, and often riddled with conflict, Congress is easily either ignored or criticized by the press. Negative and superficial congressional coverage is nothing new. But in recent years, the extent and tone have become more severe, more disturbing. The most recent accounts focus on allegations of unethical and possibly illegal conduct by members of Congress. Many reports resort to humiliating caricature.

This study supports the findings of many other accounts of how the media cover Congress. Charles Tidmarch and John Pitney analyzed all items on Congress in ten news dailies during one month in 1978 and found that journalists focused on "conflict, malfeasance and breach of public trust."[1] "On the whole," they concluded, the press "has little good to report about Congress and its membership." Such coverage has tended to "harden the image of Congress as a defective institution."[2] A major study of the impact of newspaper coverage on public confidence in institutions, also focusing on the late 1970s, found that coverage of Congress was much more unfavorable than was coverage of either the presidency or the Supreme Court.[3] Michael Robinson and Kevin Appel's analysis of network news coverage of Congress during a five-week period in 1976 found that all news stories that presented a point of view about the institution were critical of it.[4] Even the first post-Watergate Congress failed to receive a single favorable assessment.[5] More recently, Robert Gilbert concluded that congressional coverage during the spring of 1989 emphasized scandal and further contributed to the legislature's weak reputation.[6] Norman Ornstein's study of network news reporting on Congress in 1989 concluded that two-thirds of the coverage "concerned . . . three episodes of turmoil and scandal that had little to do with the constitutionally mandated duties of Congress."[7]

Press coverage of Congress over the years has moved from healthy skepticism to outright cynicism. When Congress enacted a 25 percent pay increase for its members in 1946, for example, both the *New York Times* and *Washington Post* commented that the pay increase was needed to attract top-quality people to public service and that political leaders must be paid a salary commensurate with the responsibilities of public service. The few criticisms of the raise emphasized either the principle of public service as its own reward or the need for an even larger pay increase. The press did not lead a drumbeat of criticism of Congress for enacting a pay increase, as it has in recent years.

More recently, however, the story has been far different. The press has skewered Congress for enacting pay increases. To believe the modern reporter, legislators are egregiously overpaid, indulged, and indifferent to the problems of constituents who lack six-figure incomes and fantastic job perquisites. The press portrays the nation's legislators as self-interested, self-indulgent politicians who exploit the legislative process for personal gain.

SOURCES OF NEGATIVE COVERAGE

To answer the question of how Congress can try to set the record straight, one must first explain why press coverage of Congress is so harsh. As this study shows, press coverage of Congress focuses on scandal, partisan rivalry, and interbranch conflict rather than the more complex subjects such as process and institutional concerns. The emphasis on such controversies as Rubbergate and Lunchgate underscores this problem.

Many studies have speculated about the reasons for the intense interest in scandal, rivalry, and conflict. A partial explanation is the emergence of a more aggressive, scandal-conscious news media after Watergate. Thomas Dye and Harmon Zeigler pointed to "a post-Watergate code of ethics" in which journalists seek out scandal and delve into the personal lives of public figures and other areas once considered off limits to reporters.[8] Norman Ornstein also noted that a new generation of investigative reporters, inspired by Watergate sleuths Bob Woodward and Carl Bernstein, had "accentuated and refocused the media coverage of Congress" toward "scandal and sloth."[9]

The journalists themselves confirm this tendency. A Times-Mirror survey in 1995 found that two-thirds of journalists downplay good news and spend "too much time on the failures of public officials." Many journalists fear being perceived by their colleagues as "in the tank" with politicians, wrote *U.S. News*'s Gloria Borger. Consequently, "For the press, good news is not news."[10] According to Ellen Hume, formerly of the *Wall Street Journal*, "Journalists usually err on the side of negativity."[11]

Furthermore, journalists are all too aware that conflict and scandal interest the public. Intense competition within the print media—which more recently have seen declining revenues—has driven many journalists toward increased scandal coverage to satisfy public appetites.

A great misfortune of this tendency has been the trend among the elite press to exhibit some of the same tawdry characteristics of the tabloids. As Mann and Ornstein lamented, "The prestige news outlets have adopted the sensationalist approach of their less reputable counterparts. Coverage of the House bank scandal, for example, was as overdone in the *Washington Post* as it was on radio talk shows."[12]

At one point in 1995, some members of Congress decided to strike back. Disgusted at constant media digging into their financial affairs, the Senate passed a nonbinding resolution requiring reporters covering Capitol Hill to file financial disclosures. Senators accused the correspondents of hypocrisy because many who had reported on conflicts of interests in Congress had themselves accepted honoraria for speeches before lobbying and corporate groups.[13]

Scandal, rivalry, and conflict may also be emphasized because the legislative process is tedious—"the very driest form of human endeavor," as Senator Alan Simpson once said.[14] Consequently, reporters avoid writing process and policy stories except when they are related to interbranch conflicts, rivalries among colorful personalities on Capitol Hill, or scandal. William Safire explained that editors instruct reporters to avoid "MEGOs": stories that make "my eyes glaze over."[15] Stephen Hess examined one hundred Congress stories in the *New York Times* in 1991. Only five were process-oriented stories.[16]

David Broder admitted that personal scandals are exciting and interesting; stories about institutional reform will put reporters to sleep before they get to the typewriter.[17] According to Broder, a reporter will have an easier time selling to his editor a story of petty scandal than a good many "stories of larger consequence." Junket stories sell to editors "because they fit [editors'] stereotypes of graft and sin on Capitol Hill."[18]

Both Broder and William Raspberry have written that the public holds Congress in such low esteem, in part, because of the journalistic trend of emphasizing conflict and controversy over substance. They cited the example of a vitally important job-training bill in late 1995 with little news coverage. The legislation attracted so little attention because it lacked serious opposition, and there was therefore no conflict to report.[19]

The press thus has difficulty conveying the complexities of the legislative process. The magnitude of coverage devoted to such exceptionally important events as legislative reorganization efforts and ethics reform never matches the number of stories devoted to a House bank controversy. To the extent that the press does cover procedural issues, it seems to do so when they are related to scandals and can be explained in terms of, and as reactions to, interbranch, partisan, or personal rivalries. Coverage of congressional activism during the Watergate crisis is a good example.

According to S. Robert Lichter and Daniel R. Amundson, this tendency among the print media is evident in television coverage of Congress as well. They examined comprehensively the three major networks' coverage of Congress during the period 1972–1992. They found that the coverage increasingly has focused on scandal, with decreasing emphasis on process and policy. "The news," they write, "has also increasingly emphasized conflict, both within Congress and between the institution and other participants in political affairs. . . . [T]he tone of coverage was already derogatory a generation ago and has become worse."[20]

The negativity and narrow focus of coverage are particularly important because, as Herb Asher commented, "everything that people learn about Congress is mediated."[21] There seems to be a link between the nature of congressional coverage and poor public understanding of the legislative process. Charles O. Jones looked at media coverage of a particularly busy week on Capitol Hill and found that even though the legislature had undertaken some important activities, "the American people learned hardly a smidgen about congressional action that directly affected them."[22] "Turning specifically to the committees, one does not have to wonder why the public knows so little of this ceaseless activity on Capitol Hill. The answer is that very little attention is paid to it in the press."[23]

Dye and Zeigler described coverage of Congress as "almost without exception demeaning. As a result, people regard the *institution* of Congress with cynicism and mistrust." Furthermore, "The public knows very little about Congress in its abstract, institutional form."[24] Mary Russell also found that the lack of public knowledge of Congress was due to sensational news and the press's failure to cover procedures, rules, and long-range activity.[25]

The findings here support the contention that coverage of legislative reorganization plans and other institutional matters was sparse and lacked depth. In addition to being less exciting than petty scandal, institutional stories are more complicated for reporters and editors to understand and to write about in single news stories and columns.

Besides, the presidency is the focus of Washington journalism. Congressional lawmaking is covered from the vantage of how the legislature is responding to presidential initiatives. The press perceives Congress as generally incapable of leadership. Thus in normal circumstances, Congress works best under the guiding hand of a strong president attuned to the national interest and willing to move the government in an activist, progressive direction. Members of Congress, in the minds of reporters, are primarily concerned with parochial issues. During such extraordinary periods as the Great Society and Watergate, press coverage focused more on the presidency than on Congress.

A partial explanation is the difficulty of identifying a focal point in Congress. The presidency, by contrast, is easily personalized. The focus is the president. Congress lacks a single voice. It presents a cacophony of perspectives, often in conflict. As political scientist Richard Davis wrote: "Its bicameral structure and the partisan divisions in both houses ensure that at least four leaders will compete for the role of congressional spokesperson, and the profusion of congressional committees and subcommittees . . . adds to the confusion."[26] Communications scholars Robert Denton and Gary Woodward added that whereas the presidency can, if presented effectively, appear unified, "the Congress, by contrast, is more a place of arguments, political negotiation, and compromise."[27]

Congressional coverage also suffers because of intense media interest in the horse race of presidential campaigns. In June 1995, nearly eight months before the first presidential primary of 1996, Howard Kurtz found that the media's interest in the campaign was high, whereas their interest in the governing process remained low. Reporter Gloria Borger candidly admitted, "We don't have anything very interesting to write about these days. The other choice is covering the budget, and nobody wants to write about that."[28] Yet later that year, enormous media interest turned to the budget stalemate— a story easily personalized as a rivalry between the GOP congressional leaders and President Clinton that oftentimes seemed petty.

In unusual circumstances—an executive-branch scandal, an imminent war—the news media expect Congress to adopt a more independent and activist role. Congress received a good deal of press criticism during the early stages of Watergate and Iran-contra for allegedly not acting quickly or vigorously enough to investigate the scandals. Similarly, the press criticized Congress during the early phase of the 1990–1991 Middle East crisis for not asserting its constitutional warmaking powers.

But there were the rare conditions under which Congress received press acclaim. Efforts to reform internal congressional procedures to make the legislative process more efficient, though not thoroughly reported, were treated well. The press frequently implored Congress to adopt substantially reformed ethics laws. For the periods of time covered here, Congress received the most favorable coverage when it aggressively asserted its policymaking and investigatory powers.

The 89th Congress, 1st session (1965), comes as close as can be expected to reporters' ideal Congress. They believed that Congress acted efficiently because it stretched the limits of its lawmaking powers and accepted the guiding hand of a strong, progressive president. They also supported its most activist phases during Watergate and the Middle East crisis. But the failure of an activist President Carter and Congress to work together effectively to enact progressive policies and reforms drew loud criticism.

The press's image of what Congress should be is clearly incompatible with the traditional role of the legislative branch. There is a strong press preference for a reform-oriented, progressive, policy-activist Congress that works effectively with an activist, strong president. During a congressional studies conference at the American Enterprise Institute in May 1993, a number of journalists confirmed this finding. One argued that Congress deserves praise "when Congress acts," especially when the institution displays "heroism" and policy innovation. Several colleagues agreed.[29]

Yet the Constitution's framers designed Congress to frustrate the popular will as necessary, to *not* act in an efficient, innovative fashion. Consequently, the drumbeat of press criticism, interrupted occasionally by favorable coverage during unusual circumstances, helps explain the disjunction between the legislature's intended constitutional role and journalistic expectations. No wonder Congress is held in such low public esteem when the press criticizes the institution for behaving as the Constitution's framers intended it to and then focuses on petty scandal and members' peccadilloes to the exclusion of examining process and policy.

One reporter identified his criteria for deciding whether to write a Congress story: first, the element of drama, which satisfies the public desire for "a good show"; second, the chance to feature colorful legislators who can turn a good phrase or take a bold action; third, the involvement of congressional pork, which excites public concern about whether legislators are doing their jobs. The enactment of "sound public policy" was a weak fourth. This reporter's criteria do not seem at all unusual given the nature of congressional coverage I have described.

WHAT CAN BE DONE?

The remedy for the inadequacies and distortions of congressional coverage is either for Congress to change or for the press to change. Neither is likely to change very much. But both institutions can take steps to ameliorate the problem.

Congress needs to do a better job at educating the press and the public about its activities—what it does and why it does what it does. Otherwise, journalists and the public will continue to harbor expectations—routine efficiency, activist policymaking, large-scale internal reform, strong leadership during crises and when the president is under siege—that the institution generally is not designed to live up to.

Congress also does a poor job of protecting its image. In Richard Fenno's classic argument, members "run *for* Congress by running *against* Congress."[30] In their districts, they reinforce unfavorable opinions of the institution so that they can distance themselves from it and by implication assume the virtues that it supposedly lacks. Even electorally safe incumbents do not educate constituents about the strengths of their institution. Instead, they attack it as a way of protecting themselves politically.[31] Michael Robinson and Kevin Appel have also noted that members of the legislature "complain about Congress and praise themselves as individuals."[32] James McCartney of Knight-Ridder commented, "Congress does a lousy job in telling a reporter what goes on. The problem with Congress is that it has no organization and is just babble. It needs to present its information better, like the White House."[33]

Congress needs an office of public information, much like the White House office of communications, devoted to dispensing information about its duties and activities. Government organizations need such entities to improve the flow of information to the public, and Congress should not be an exception.[34] Although Congress has expanded and improved in-house media operations to help meet the needs of individual members to communicate with constituents, it has been less active in meeting more general and institutional needs.[35] Some public anger can be overcome if Congress would take more seriously the need to educate the public about the nature and limitations of the legislative process. Politically aware citizens today are learning about Congress's activities through media coverage. An office of public information can offer those citizens a different perspective on how the Congress works.

Individual members can also orient their own behavior in a way that better protects the institutional reputation. Electorally safe members—a large group indeed—have the leeway to educate constituents properly about the Congress and take some responsibility for its actions.[36] Timothy Cook suggested that members can work better with journalistic definitions of newsworthiness by explaining complex issues and activities in a clear, comprehensible fashion.[37] Members could also do a better job of lowering constituents' expectations of legislative performance and avoiding conflicts that generate short-term publicity and political gain at the expense of Congress's image.

Mann and Ornstein suggested a number of other innovations that could enhance media and public understanding of Congress. For example, they would like to see the creation of a visitors' center in the Capitol modeled after the one in Colonial Williamsburg. The idea is to provide a starting point for visitors to become oriented about the history and workings of the legislative process. They advocated a second capitol tour—one that gives visitors a better understanding of the legislative process. Furthermore, visitors to the House and Senate galleries can be given a more meaningful experience with some additional guidance—better literature about the floor, a guide to the debate on the floor, and earphones in the seats to provide commentary on floor action. C-SPAN viewers could learn more about Congress if, instead of background music during votes, members could come off the floor to explain on-camera the events of the day.[38]

Finally, responsibility for presenting a balanced and realistic representation of Congress lies with the journalists. In 1975, former Senator J. William Fulbright (D–Ark.) wrote that "the national press would do well to reconsider its priorities. It has excelled in exposing . . . the high crimes and peccadilloes of persons in high places. But it has fallen short—far short—in its higher responsibility of public education."[39] Schools of journalism could play a most positive role if, in addition to training students in the craft of journalism, they also educated future political reporters about the nature of the governing process.

The problem today is far worse than described by Fulbright. Much of the reporting and commentary on Congress from the prestige press has a tabloid quality. The consequences of such Congress bashing are clear enough: public anger at the legislative branch and cynicism, the inability of Congress to do its job effectively, increased rates of retirement from Congress, the refusal of many outstanding citizens to serve there, and a possible crisis of legitimacy for the institution.

It is difficult to imagine that congressional coverage will deemphasize controversy, scandal, and intrigue and focus on process and policy very soon. But reporters and editors can voluntarily do a better job of educating the public about Congress and representative government. Whether they are motivated by concern over the impact of fueling public cynicism toward the institution or by professional pride in factual and fair-minded reporting, journalists could truly serve the public by covering the legislative branch in a manner that befits the most representative institution of our government.

NOTES

1. Charles M. Tidmarch and John J. Pitney, Jr., "Covering Congress," *Polity* 17 (Spring 1985): 482.

2. Ibid., p. 481.

3. Arthur Miller, Edie Goldenberg, and Lutz Erbring, "Type-set Politics: Impact of Newspapers on Public Confidence," *American Political Science Review* 73 (March 1979): 70.

4. Michael J. Robinson and Kevin R. Appel, "Network News Coverage of Congress," *Political Science Quarterly 94 (Fall 1979): 412.*

5. Ibid., 417.

6. Robert E. Gilbert, "President versus Congress: The Struggle for Public Attention," *Congress and the Presidency* 16 (Autumn 1989): 99.

7. Norman Ornstein, "What TV News Doesn't Report about Congress—and Should," *TV Guide* 37 (October 21, 1989), p. 11.

8. Thomas R. Dye and Harmon Zeigler, *American Politics in the Media Age*, 2d ed. (Monterey, CA: Brooks/Cole, 1986), p. 212.

9. Norman J. Ornstein, "The Open Congress Meets the President," in Anthony King, ed., *Both Ends of the Avenue: The Presidency, the Executive Branch, and Congress in the 1980s* (Washington, DC: American Enterprise Institute, 1983), p. 201.

10. Gloria Borger, "Cynicism and Tankophobia," *U.S. News and World Report*, June 5, 1995, p. 34.

11. Quoted in Stephen Hess, "The Decline and Fall of Congressional News," in Thomas Mann and Norman Ornstein, eds., *Congress, the Press, and the Public.* (Washington, DC: Brookings/American Enterprise Institute, 1994), p. 149.

12. Thomas Mann and Norman Ornstein, "Introduction," in Mann and Ornstein, *Congress, the Press, and the Public*, p. 8.

13. Howard Kurtz, "Senate Eyes Reporters' Honoraria," *Washington Post*, July 21, 1995, pp. C1, C4.

14. Quoted in Greg Schneiders, "The 90–Second Handicap: Why TV Coverage of Legislation Falls Short," *Washington Journalism Review*, June 1985, p. 44.

15. William Safire, "The MEGO News Era," *Washington Star*, September 6, 1973, p. A15.

16. Hess, "Decline and Fall of Congressional News," p. 150.

17. David Broder, *Behind the Front Page: A Candid Look at How the News Is Made* (New York: Simon & Schuster, 1987), p. 216.

18. Ibid., p. 227.

19. William Raspberry, "Blow-by-Blow Coverage," *Washington Post*, October 30, 1995, p. A17.

20. S. Robert Lichter and Daniel R. Amundson, "Less News Is Worse News: Television News Coverage of Congress, 1972–1992," in Mann and Ornstein, *Congress, the Press, and the Public*, p. 139.

21. Herb Asher panel discussion comment. Brookings Institution/American Enterprise Institute Conference on "Congress, the Press and the Public," Washington, DC, May 1993. Attended by author.

22. Charles O. Jones, *The United States Congress: People, Place, and Policy* (Homewood, IL: Dorsey, 1982) p. 48.

23. Ibid., p. 46.

24. Dye and Zeigler, *American Politics in the Media Age*, pp. 211–212.

25. Mary Russell, "The Press and the Committee System," in Doris A. Graber, ed., *Media Power in Politics* (Washington, DC: Congressional Quarterly, 1984), p. 228.

26. Richard Davis, *The Press and American Politics: The New Mediator* (New York: Longman, 1992), p. 161.

27. Robert E. Denton, Jr., and Gary C. Woodward, *Political Communication in America*, 2d ed. (New York: Praeger, 1990), p. 284.

28. Howard Kurtz, "Hot Tips on the Horse-Race to Nowhere," *Washington Post*, June 25, 1995, pp. C1, C2.

29. "Congress, the Press, and the Public." Conference cosponsored by the Brookings Institution and the American Enterprise Institute, Washington, DC, May 1993. Attended by author.

30. Richard F. Fenno, Jr., *Home Style: House Members in Their Districts* (Boston: Little, Brown, 1978), p. 168.

31. Ibid., pp. 246–247.

32. Robinson and Appel, "Network News Coverage of Congress," p. 416.

33. Quoted in Davis, *Press and American Politics*, p. 170.

34. Congress has a Legislative Information Office (LIO) that cannot serve the function of explaining the institution and its procedures. The LIO can inform people—at least those who are both familiar with the office and motivated to use it—about pending legislation and the status of matters being considered by Congress. It is prohibited from identifying members by party or providing the partisan breakdown of a vote on a bill.

35. Michael J. Robinson, "Three Faces of Congressional Media," in Thomas Mann and Norman Ornstein, eds., *The New Congress* (Washington, DC: American Enterprise Institute, 1981), p. 64.

36. Fenno, *Home Style*, p. 246.

37. Timothy Cook, *Making Laws and Making News: Media Strategies in the U.S. House of Representatives* (Washington, DC: Brookings, 1989), p. 170.

38. Mann and Ornstein, "Introduction," in Mann and Ornstein, *Congress, the Press, and the Public*, pp. 10–13.

39. Quoted in Broder, *Behind the Front Page*, p. 213.

Selected Bibliography

Bayley, Edwin. *Joe McCarthy and the Press*. Madison: University of Wisconsin Press, 1981.

Broder, David S. *Behind the Front Page: A Candid Look at How the News Is Made*. New York: Simon & Schuster, 1987.

Congressional Quarterly. *Origins and Development of Congress*. Washington, DC: Congressional Quarterly, 1976.

Cook, Timothy. *Making Laws and Making News: Media Strategies in the U.S. House of Representatives*. Washington, DC: Brookings, 1989.

Davis, Richard. *The Press and American Politics: The New Mediator.* New York: Longman, 1992.

Denton, Robert E., Jr., and Gary C. Woodward. *Political Communication in America*. 2d ed. New York: Praeger, 1990.

Dye, Thomas R., and Harmon Zeigler. *American Politics in the Media Age*. 2d ed. Monterey, CA: Brooks/Cole, 1986.

Edwards, George C. *The Public Presidency: The Pursuit of Popular Support*. New York: St. Martin's, 1983.

Fenno, Richard F., Jr. *Home Style: House Members in Their Districts*. Boston: Little, Brown, 1978.

Gilbert, Robert E. "President versus Congress: The Struggle for Public Attention." *Congress and the Presidency* 16 (Autumn 1989): 83–102.

Graber, Doris A., ed. *Media Power in Politics*. Washington, DC: Congressional Quarterly, 1984.

Hess, Stephen. *The Government/Press Connection*. Washington, DC: Brookings, 1984.

————. *The Washington Reporters*. Washington, DC: Brookings, 1981.

Jones, Charles O. *The United States Congress: People, Place, and Policy*. Homewood, IL: Dorsey, 1982.

————. *The Reagan Legacy: Promise and Performance.* Chatham, NJ: Chatham House, 1988.

King, Anthony, ed. *Both Ends of the Avenue: The Presidency, the Executive Branch, and Congress in the 1980s.* Washington, DC: American Enterprise Institute, 1983.

Mann, Thomas, and Norman Ornstein, eds. *Congress, the Press, and the Public.* Washington, DC: Brookings/American Enterprise Institute, 1994.

————, eds. *The New Congress.* Washington, DC: American Enterprise Institute, 1981.

Miller, Arthur, Edie Goldenberg, and Lutz Erbring. "Type-set Politics: Impact of Newspapers on Public Confidence." *American Political Science Review* 73 (March 1979): 67–84.

Oleszek, Walter J. *Congressional Procedures and the Policy Process.* Washington, DC: Congressional Quarterly, 1978.

Ornstein, Norman J. "What TV News Doesn't Report About Congress—and Should." *TV Guide* 37 (October 21, 1989): 10–13.

Robinson, Michael J., and Kevin R. Appel. "Network News Coverage of Congress." *Political Science Quarterly* 94 (Fall 1979): 407–418.

Rozell, Mark J. *The Press and the Carter Presidency.* Boulder, CO: Westview, 1989.

Tidmarch, Charles M., and John J. Pitney, Jr. "Covering Congress." *Polity* 17 (Spring 1985): 463–483.

Wilcox, Clyde. *The Latest American Revolution? The 1994 Elections and Their Implications for Governance.* New York: St. Martin's, 1995.

Index

Aid to Families with Dependent Children (AFDC), 59
Aiken, George, 33
Alexander, Lamar, 103
Alter, Jonathan, 112
American Broadcast Company (ABC), News polls, 1, 2, 4, 91–92
American Enterprise Institute (AEI), 132
American Political Science Association, 12
Amundson, Daniel R., 130
Anderson, Jack, 74
Anderson, J. W., 44
Appel, Kevin, 127, 133
Asher, Herb, 4, 130

Baker, Bobby, 32, 34
Baker, Howard, 59
Baker, Russell, 44, 111
Barr, Mike, 4
Bayley, Edwin, 17
Bendiner, Robert, 35
Berke, Richard L., 103
Bernstein, Carl, 128
Boland Amendment, 65, 67, 69, 72

Boyd, Gerald M., 64
Broder, David S., 3, 42, 61, 62, 64, 74, 75, 80, 92, 100–101, 104, 108, 109, 129–130
Bush, George, 4, 76–79, 101

Cable News Network (CNN), poll, 115
Cable Satellite Public Affairs Network (C-SPAN), 102, 134
Cannon, Lou, 56
Carlson, Margaret, 115
Carter, Jimmy, 53–56, 59, 132
Center for Media and Public Affairs, 109, 112–113
Childs, Marquis, 15, 17, 28–29
Church, George J., 79
Churchill, Winston, 79
Civil rights, 18–20, 25
Clinton, Bill, 1, 2, 102, 105, 111, 131
Clinton, Hillary Rodham, 113
Cloud, Stanley, 98–99
Cohen, Richard, 74, 114
Congress: ethics, 3, 5, 6, 11, 25, 30, 32–34, 57–58, 79, 91–101, 102, 113–114; polls and public atti-

tudes, 1, 2, 4, 5, 7, 82, 91–92, 101–102, 104, 105, 106, 111, 112–113; Republican majority, 1–2, 101–115; salary and pay raises, 12, 14–16, 32, 58, 72–76, 97, 103, 128; seniority system, 15–16, 31, 34–37
congressional elections, 1–2, 7, 101–107
Congressional Record, 34
Contract with America, 1–4, 7, 104-110
Cook, Timothy, 134
Coppola, Francis Ford, 93
Cox, Archibald, 39
Cutler, Lloyd, 72

Democratic Study Group, 35
Denton, Robert, 131
Dewar, Helen, 101
Dionne, E. J., Jr., 63, 79–80
Dodd, Thomas J., 32, 34

Economic Recovery Tax Act, 59–60
Edwards, George C., 5
Eisenhower, Dwight D., 11, 19, 28
Elving, Ronald, 8
Ervin, Sam, 38, 39, 43

Fenno, Richard, 133
Foley, Thomas J., 56, 57–58
Foley, Tom, 105, 106
Ford, Gerald R., 59, 114
Fritchey, Clayton, 40–41
Fulbright, J. William, 134

Garment, Suzanne, 66
Gergen, David, 97, 111
Gigot, Paul, 79, 100
Gilbert, Robert, 127–128
Gingrich, Newt, 3, 4, 7, 104, 110–115
Great Society, 6, 25-31, 60, 131
Greenfield, Meg, 57, 69, 100, 108, 112

Greenhouse, Linda, 66, 68
Gugliotta, Guy, 108–109

Harding, Warren, 29
Herbers, John, 55
Hess, Stephen, 9 n. 11, 129
House of Representatives: bank scandal, 91–101, 129, 130; Judiciary Committee, 38, 42, 43, 44, 46; Post Office controversy, 102
Hume, Ellen, 129
Humphrey, Gordon, 73
Hunt, Albert R., 55

Ignatius, David, 69
Iran-contra investigations, 7, 65-72, 131
Ito, Lance, 4

Johnson, Haynes, 61, 70, 100
Johnson, Lyndon B., 18–20, 25–30, 78
Joint Budget Committee, 12
Joint Committee on the Organization of Congress, 12–16
Jones, Charles O., 59, 130

Keating, Charles, 92, 99
Keating Five, 92–95, 99
Kefauver, Estes, 16
Kennedy, John F., 55, 79
Kenworthy, Tom, 99
Kerrey, Bob, 104
Kilpatrick, James, 66
Klein, Joe, 106
Knight-Ridder, 133
Kraft, Joseph, 44, 56, 57
Kramer, Michael, 98
Krauthammer, Charles, 67, 74, 77, 109
Krock, Arthur, 27
Kurtz, Howard, 131

La Follette, Robert M., Jr., 12, 13, 14, 31
Landauer, Jerry, 33–34
Lawrence, David, 37
Legislative Information Office (LIO), 136
Legislative Reorganization Act (1946), 6, 11, 12–16
Legislative Reorganization Act (1970), 6, 25, 34–37
Lewis, Anthony, 42, 76
Lichter, S. Robert, 130
Limbaugh, Rush, 106
Lincoln Savings and Loan, 92

Mann, Judy, 74
Mann, Thomas, 129, 134
Marder, Murrey, 17
McCarthy, Colman, 74
McCarthy, Joseph, 6, 16–17
McCartney, James, 133
McGrory, Mary, 68–69, 78, 100, 109, 111
McHugh, Matthew, 101
Medicaid, 59
Medicare, 25, 26, 27, 59
Meet the Press, 113
Middle East crisis (1990–1991), 76–81, 131
Moley, Raymond, 13, 15, 16, 31
Mondale, Walter, 54
Monroney, A. S. Mike., 12, 13, 14, 31
Morgan, Dan, 67

Nader, Ralph, 73
Nash, Nathaniel C., 77
Naughton, James, 38
Newsweek, 5, 13, 37, 41, 42, 43, 44, 56, 63, 69, 73, 91, 96–97, 105, 106, 109, 115
New York Daily News, 114
New York Times, 5, 13, 16, 17, 18–19, 26–31, 33, 35, 36–37, 38–39, 40, 41, 42, 43, 44, 54, 55, 59–60, 63, 64, 66, 70, 75, 78–79, 91, 93–94, 101, 104, 105–106, 110, 128, 129
Nixon, Richard M., 37–47, 53, 61
North American Free Trade Agreement (NAFTA), 4
North, Oliver, 65-70
Novak, Robert, 29, 63, 98, 108, 109

Oakes, John B., 17
Office of Price Administration, 14
O'Neill, Thomas P. (Tip), 64
Ornstein, Norman, 128, 129, 134

Packwood, Bob, 3, 63, 111
Parshall, Gerald, 56
Pearson, Drew, 17, 29
Persian Gulf War, 76–81, 131
Pitney, John, 127
Podhoretz, Norman, 66
Poindexter, John, 65-67
Powell, Adam Clayton, 32, 34

Quayle, Dan, 115

Raspberry, William, 42, 106, 114, 129–130
Reagan, Ronald, 4, 7, 58–66, 68, 71, 72
Reston, James, 28, 69
Roberts, Steven V., 61, 64, 66, 106, 107
Robinson, Michael, 127, 133
Rodino Committee. *See* House of Representatives, Judiciary Committee
Rodino, Peter, 38, 42, 44
Roosevelt, Franklin D., 6, 11, 12, 28, 79
Roschco, Bernard, 17
Rosenbaum, David E., 43, 63
Rostenkowski, Dan, 64, 103

Rowen, Hobart, 61
Royster, Vermont, 38
Rule XXII, 18
Rule 43, 32
Rule 44, 32
Russell, Mary, 130

Safire, William, 100
Samuelson, Robert J., 106, 109
Saturday Night Massacre, 40
Seib, Gerald F., 104
Senate: civil rights, 18–20; crime investigation committee, 16; Ethics Committee, 94-95, 99; Select Committee on Watergate, 38–41, 43
Shannon, William V., 35–36
Shapiro, Walter, 73
Shaw, Donald, 4
Simpson, Alan, 129
Simpson, O. J., 4
Social Security, 59
Stockman, David, 62
Stone, Marvin, 58

Taft-Hartley Act, 30
Term limits, 98, 107–108
Thomas, Clarence, 92
Tidmarch, Charles, 127
Time, 5, 34, 43, 46, 57, 73, 95–96, 98–99, 104, 105, 106, 111, 114, 115
Times-Mirror, 128–129
Tolchin, Martin, 61
Toner, Robin, 79
Tower Commission, 67
Truman, Harry S, 12

U.N. Resolution 678, 76
U.S. News and World Report, 5, 14, 37, 46, 54–55, 56, 57, 58, 64, 71–72, 73–74, 97, 102, 110, 115, 129

Van Atta, Dale, 74

Waldholtz, Enid, 111
Wall Street Journal, 5, 14, 15, 17, 26, 30, 31, 33, 35, 38, 39, 41, 42, 55, 58, 60, 61–62, 64, 66–67, 71, 74, 75, 79, 92–93, 95, 102, 104, 107, 108, 109, 110, 112, 129
War Powers Act, 46
Washington Post, 1, 5, 13–14, 16, 17, 18–20, 26, 29, 31, 33, 36, 38, 39, 40, 44, 58, 61, 63, 65, 67, 68, 75, 78, 79, 91–92, 95, 97, 99, 102, 103, 105–106, 107, 108, 109, 110, 111, 112, 128, 129
Watergate, 6, 25, 38–47, 56, 57, 65, 128, 131, 132
White, Jack E., 112
White, William S., 28, 43
Whitewater, 111
Wicker, Tom, 27, 28, 29, 43, 54, 63–64, 65–66
Wilcox, Clyde, 2
Will, George F., 61, 66–67, 76–77, 98, 103
Wirthlin Group Poll, 1–2
Woodward, Bob, 128
Woodward, Gary, 131
Wright, James, 73, 114

Zeigler, Harmon, 128, 130
Zuckerman, Mortimer B., 71–72, 106

About the Author

MARK J. ROZELL is a Lecturer in the Catholic University graduate program in congressional studies. He is the author of six books including *The Press and the Bush Presidency* (Praeger, 1996).